deve...

matters

...hown below.

To the memory of the Revd Canon Dr Susan Cole King
1934 – 2001

development matters

Christian perspectives on globalization

edited by Charles Reed

CHURCH HOUSE
PUBLISHING

Church House Publishing
Church House
Great Smith Street
London SW1P 3NZ

ISBN 0 7151 6588 7

GS Misc 634

Designed by Visible Edge

Typeset in Franklin Gothic 9pt

Cover design by Visible Edge

Cover photograph: View of Medellin
from Mano de Dios. P. Jones
Griffiths/Christian Aid/Magnum.

Printed by MPG Books Ltd
Bodmin, Cornwall

Published 2001 for the Board for
Social Responsibility of the Church of
England by Church House Publishing

*Copyright © The Archbishops' Council
2001*

contents

contents

contributors

Andrew Davey is an Assistant Secretary in the Church of England's Board for Social Responsibility, with particular responsibility for urban affairs and racial justice issues. He experienced a transnational theological education, including studies at Westcott House; The Urban Theology Unit, Sheffield; Tamilnadu Theological Seminary, India; and The Ecumenical Institute, Bossey. For five years he was Vicar of St Luke's Church, North Peckham. His doctoral work examined the Faith in the City process from a liberationist perspective. He is currently working on an urban primer, to be published by SPCK.

David Gosling trained as a nuclear physicist prior to ordination. He has worked extensively on environmental issues in developing countries, and has been Director of Church and Society of the World Council of Churches. He is currently a member and former Fellow of Clare Hall and a member of the Faculty of Divinity in the University of Cambridge. He is also an environmental consultant to USPG.

Ian Linden has been Director of the Catholic Institute for International Relations (CIIR) since 1986 having worked on its southern Africa desk for seven years. A writer and broadcaster who has lived and taught in Malawi and Nigeria, he has published four books on aspects of Christianity and Islam in Africa, and many articles on social justice stemming from aspects of CIIR's work.

Peter Malcolm has worked for the CBI for over 35 years, following a few years' industrial experience in administration and finance. His CBI appointments have included Assistant Director in the regions, Head of Membership Relations, Senior Policy Adviser on trade and investment throughout the GATT Uruguay Round, and Head of General International Policy covering trade promotion and facilitation, international development, customs policy and procedures, export finance and controls. He is Secretary of the International Committee, which oversees all the CBI's international work and sub-groups.

Claire Melamed is a Senior Policy Officer at Christian Aid, working on international trade and globalization. Before joining Christian Aid in 1998, she gained a PhD at the University of London, researching the impact of foreign investment in the cotton sector in Mozambique. She has also taught on an MSc course in Development Studies, worked for the United Nations in Mozambique, and published books and articles on structural adjustment, investment and trade.

John Montagu, the Earl of Sandwich, has been a member of the House of Lords since 1995. He is a freelance editor and consultant to several international aid agencies such as Save the Children, CARE, and Christian Aid. He has a wide knowledge of voluntary organizations in Asia and West Africa. He has published and edited several books on international development, which reflects his broad interest in issues such as child labour, Aids and education.

Daleep Mukarji is currently Director of Christian Aid. He has worked on rural health and development programmes in India and was General Secretary to the Christian Medical Association of India from 1985 to 1994. He was Secretary of Health, Community and Justice at the World Council of Churches in Geneva from 1994 until 1998, when he moved to London to become Director of Christian Aid. He is the current Chairman of the British Overseas Aid Group and the Association of Church Related Development Agencies Europe.

Mark Oxbrow is Mission Consultant for the Church Mission Society (CMS) and currently serves as their Director for Mission in Europe. He is Chair of the Europe Mission Forum of the Churches Commission on Mission (CCOM) and a Council Member of Global Connections (formerly EMA). Before joining CMS in 1988 he served in parishes in Rochester and Newcastle dioceses and worked with the National Health Service developing community chaplaincy for the mentally ill.

Gillian Paterson is a consultant on development and health issues, and a writer. She worked for Christian Aid for many years, and was Mission Education Secretary at the Council of Churches for Britain and Ireland. Recent books include *Love in a Time of AIDS* (Risk, 1997); *Still Flowing: Women, Church and God* (Risk, 1999); and *Church and HIV/AIDS in Sub-Saharan Africa* (Christian Aid, 2001).

Jennifer Potter grew up in Yorkshire but has spent most of her adult life working as a geography and environmental science teacher in southern Africa, mostly in Botswana. For many years she was active in the Christian Council in Botswana and was the Acting General Secretary for a period in the mid-1990s. On returning to Britain in 1996 she took up her current post as Secretary for International Affairs for the Methodist Church.

Charles Reed studied at the London School of Economics and at Trinity Hall, Cambridge, where he completed his doctorate in European Political Science. He has worked as a research consultant to the European Commission (Directorate General 1) and to the Runnymede Trust's Commission for the Creation of a Multi-Ethnic Britain. He worked as a Public Affairs Consultant to Burson Marsteller prior to becoming the International and Development Affairs Secretary to the Church of England's Board for Social Responsibility in 1998. In March 2000 he was seconded to the United Nations Development Programme in Iraq.

Peter Selby is the Bishop of Worcester. Most of his ordained ministry has been in the field of adult education and mission, particularly promoting lay discipleship. After serving as Canon Missioner in Newcastle upon Tyne and as Suffragan Bishop of Kingston he became the William Leech Professorial Fellow in Applied Christian Theology at Newcastle University and undertook research into the Christian meaning of the world of credit and debt. He is the author of *Grace and Mortgage* (Darton, Longman and Todd, 1997).

Wendy Tyndale has been working on human rights and development issues since 1973, mainly in Latin America. In 1998 she became the Co-ordinator of the World Faiths Development Dialogue, which was set up by Dr George Carey, the Archbishop of Canterbury, and James D. Wolfensohn, President of the World Bank, as a dialogue among people of the world's religions and between them and the international financial institutions and multilateral agencies.

Kevin Ward studied at Edinburgh University and at Trinity College, Cambridge, where he worked for his doctorate in African studies. He worked in Africa from 1969 to 1990, as a teacher in Kenya and, from 1976, as a theological educator in Uganda at the Bishop Tucker Theological College. He was ordained in the Church of Uganda. From 1991 to 1995 he served as a parish priest in Halifax and officer for the Diocese of Wakefield's link with the Diocese of Mara in Tanzania. Since 1995 he has lectured in African Religious Studies in the Department of Theology and Religious Studies of the University of Leeds.

Karl Ziegler is the London-based Director of the Centre for Accountability and Debt Relief. He serves also as a Chief Executive of the Kinnerton Research Centre and is a Director of Transparency International. Educated at Andover, Yale and the Harvard Business School, he spent 17 years in international banking.

foreword

The process that produced this report for the General Synod differs from the more usual method of a working party set up by a board or council. The Board for Social Responsibility has excellent relationships with development agencies such as Christian Aid and CAFOD, and with those mission agencies active in development. In addition, the Board for Social Responsibility has an extensive network with the dioceses through its Social Responsibility Officers, World Development Advisors, and Diocesan Link Officers. The International and Development Affairs Committee, chaired by the Bishop of Selby, therefore decided to invite some of these people to contribute to a collection of essays offering Christian reflections on globalization from the perspective of international development. The purpose is to help members of General Synod, and the wider general public, grapple with the complexity of globalization and to understand what measures they can take to ensure that this phenomenon works to the benefit rather than to the detriment of those most vulnerable within our global village. We are grateful to all those who contributed essays in the midst of busy lives. This collection is authorized by the Board for Social Responsibility as a contribution to debate, but the board does not endorse the views expressed by individual contributors.

✠ Tom Butler
Bishop of Southwark
Chair, Board for Social Responsibility

introduction

This collection of essays has been produced about the same time as
HM Government's second White Paper on international development,
Eliminating World Poverty: Making Globalisation Work for the Poor which
was published in December 2000. It has been designed to be read alongside the White Paper offering comments from distinctively Christian points
of view on many of the issues raised in it.Manifestly this is a critical
moment in development matters. The formal winding-up of Jubilee 2000
presents Christians and many others with a new set of challenges and
opportunities. The Government sees the main challenge as grasping the
opportunities afforded by globalisation to eliminate world poverty, 'the
greatest moral challenge facing our generation'. For many people, however,
it is unfettered globalisation of trade, which threatens to exacerbate, rather
than promising an end to, world poverty. A good many such issues come
up in the pages which follow and I hope that reading and debating them will
lead towards a deepening understanding of the sort of action that really is
good news for the world's poor.

✠ Humphrey Taylor
Bishop of Selby
Chair, International and Development Affairs Committee

part I
the Church, globalization and development

chapter 1
globalization and the Church: an overview

Ian Linden

introduction

Certain words powerfully influence the way that we look both at historical periods and at the world. They do so by summing up a compelling contemporary story in which people find meaning or make their own. The text of such stories is invariably open to a number of different interpretations; a superficially universal account of how the world stands is subtly interwoven with particular and political understandings. Today the word 'globalization' encapsulates our latest contemporary story.

When the final chapter of the Cold War ended – in 1989 – the short twentieth century was deemed to have come to a close. A cognitive map had become redundant. International relations suffered a temporary loss of meaning and there was a mood of transition. With the growing acceptance of globalization as a framework for understanding the structure of our world, and as a new reading of the signs of the times, we shifted from one epoch to another. The old order of a bipolar world dominated by geopolitics disappeared to give way to a unipolar world dominated by geo-economics. A new story with its one-word summary, 'globalization', contended with others, most notably Samuel Huntington's 'clash of civilizations' and 'civil society'.[1] But 'globalization' moved slowly centre-stage – with 'civil society' not far behind – and now is the common currency of much debate.

The idea of globalization was dominated from the beginning by the story of the 'global economy', the dramatic expansion in the mobility of finance and investment – private investment up from $44 billion in 1990 to $164 billion in 1998 – and, to a lesser extent, trade, and what this meant. For the realm of the economic had begun to dominate public discourse, and a particular set of economic prescriptions and ideas had taken on a hegemonic nature, uncontested, coercive, almost common sense. The idea of globalization, however, suggested a more complex story, a wider and increasing interconnectedness of individuals, organizations, and corporations, and the growth of embryonic and genuinely global institutions that were more than the international bodies that emerged from the ashes of the Second World War.

So it is not far-fetched to suggest with John Gray in *False Dawn* that, in this postmodern age that rejects coercive grand narratives, 'globalization' represents a last rally by European Enlightenment thought.[2] Like the Enlightenment it is seen as both a process and a set of desirable – or undesirable – policies, with process and policies not always distinguished, leading to sterile debates about inevitability.

a global economy?

There can be little doubt that the technological basis for both a global economy and nascent global institutions lay in the communications and information technology revolution whose prodigious consequences became apparent towards the end of the 1990s. Developments in microchips and fibre optics drastically reduced the cost of communication and made possible in cyberspace a massive compression of space and time. This permitted rapid mobilization of civil society with consequences seen in Seattle and Prague, or, indeed, during the European fuel disputes. This in turn brought the political dream of a global 'social contract' involving international development targets, a commitment to international equity, and a 'global civil society' into the realm of the distant but feasible. Most notably, the new technology permitted complex manufactured goods to be built from components produced in a number of different countries, in a new process of transnational production, and a dramatic increase in foreign direct investment as technical barriers to rapid – and often complex – capital flows were eliminated. The global economy became characterized by the dominance of the financial services sector of the USA and the European Union, which packaged accumulated capital, essentially savings, and shifted it rapidly around the world at a profit. Exchange of money 'surrogates' – tokens of tokens – in cyberspace could, and did, build and destroy whole economies.

The daily turnover of currency transactions in the money markets during the 1970s was about $1,000 million; it is now well above $1,000,000 million, more than a hundred times the currency reserves held by all the world's governments put together. The policy prescription needed for this process to prevail was deregulation. These prodigious currency flows further underlined Bishop Peter Selby's insight that Christianity needs to rediscover a radical critique of the meaning and role of money.[3]

Nonetheless, growth in trade in the normally accepted sense of the move-ment of goods around the world is perhaps the least significant feature of today's globalization, though the most obvious. As the European Commissioner for External Relations, Chris Patten, recently pointed out, this form of globalization is not new. John Maynard Keynes in *The Economic Consequences of Peace* wrote vividly of the 'internationalisation of social and economic life' in the years before the First World War in Britain. And although Kenyan beans and Nicaraguan coffee are noticeable on our supermarket shelves today, Keynes was equally struck by the vision of the Edwardian Londoner ordering 'the various products of the whole earth in such quantity as he might see fit' – though using the revolutionary telephone rather than the Tesco web site.[4]

In the period preceding the First World War, some 45 per cent of British wealth was then invested overseas, and in the 50 years before 1914 some 36 million people emigrated from Europe, mainly to the USA in search of employment. Indeed, the period before the First World War saw a doubling of trade, largely in bulk commodities such as cotton, sugar and coal carried in steamships, but increasingly in manufactured goods. The variety of goods traded has clearly multiplied, but a major increase in the percentage of wealth generated by trade compared to wealth generated by the domestic market is not a unique feature of today's globalization.

Moreover, it needs underlining that regionalization is as significant a feature of today's world as globalization; regional blocs and markets structure trade links. Most transnationals are regional corporations with outreach. Close scrutiny of boards of directors reveals their narrow national origins. One of the characteristics of the global economy is that it is not at present global. Investment in Africa outside of South Africa and a few countries rich in oil or mineral resources is negligible. Many African countries were no less off the economic map in 2000 than they were off the geographical map in 1500. The income of the top 10 per cent of the population in Brazil is 27 times greater than that of the bottom 40 per cent; the income of the top 1 per cent is greater than all the bottom 50 per cent added together. There is nothing as spectacular as these obscenely skewed income distributions beyond the Latin American continent. South East Asia is different again, the victim of spectacular booms, busts and bubbles. Regions matter. Economic and political culture matters.

ideology and the Church
Beyond the simple observation that the characteristic contours of today's globalization as a process grew out of the information technology revolution

– like the Reformation out of the printed word – lies an ideological morass of meanings and interpretations. Much that is claimed of globalization by one group or another turns out to be untrue, trivially true, not necessarily attributable to globalization, or admits of many exceptions. The highest aspiration imagined by the European Union for the least developed countries, for example, is to be 'inserted' – note the passive tense – smoothly into the global economy. And it is supposedly through this integration that the poorest countries will eradicate their poverty. There is something of the universal panacea here that sits ill with the catastrophic collapse of the economy of the ex-Soviet Union as it adopted neo-liberal prescriptions and attempted to integrate with the wider capitalist economy.

Likewise there is confusion about globalization's supposed drive for uniformity. The fundamental idea behind market economics is the generation of specialism and comparative advantage. Thus the typical image of the globalized economy is likely to be diversity, silicon valleys, the Finnish economy dominated by telecommunications and Nokia, and the City of London – alongside barren, desertified landscapes with starving people. True, the invasive multinationals with their uniform brand logos are no less part of the story – 'let them drink Coke' is the reality in many parts of the world where water is absent or lethally contaminated – but the natural consequence of globalization is a mixture of both striking differentiation and uniformity. All countries will not become the same. US culture will not necessarily be victorious, as anyone with more than a passing acquaintance with Asia will conclude. Many people deeply fear both cultural and economic domination.

The idea that the development of a global economy spells the dramatic decline of the power of states, gained over the past 200 years, hardly bears scrutiny. The international political architecture is still predominantly controlled by states that maintain a degree of monopoly on coercive force and many of whom are able to combat threats to sovereignty. The hegemony of the USA and its equation of global interest with its own narrow national interest is a serious political problem but one still susceptible to political solutions. While it is true that there are powerful forces undermining the modern state, this is both a convenient excuse for governments unwilling to promote democratic or pro-poor policies, and potentially a spur to both more inclusive forms of nationalism and dangerous forms of fundamentalism and identity politics.

Given the variety of ways in which globalization is described, it has to be asked whether people are talking about the same thing. 'We will do our best to bring the world together by building up the global auto-industry', Toyota has gone on record as saying. The Brazilian farmer pushed off his land by the boom in soya bean production sees globalization as destitution, exclusion and ruin. For a Japanese businessman it may mean suicide as his bank and life collapse under the tidal flows of capital in and out of Asia. For the new employees in India's burgeoning information technology industry globalization means an unexpected movement into prosperity. For a French film producer it signifies the cultural threat of the United States in the film industry. Yet, in one way or another, each might sign up to the idea that what they describe – or what they are worried about – is the uncontested triumph of a particular form of liberal capitalism.

The reality is that there are no neutral vantage points, no analysis that can escape entirely from ideological premises. Is globalization then akin to a mirage generated by overheated western economies? Yes and no. Globalization appears as a stage in the evolution of capitalism. A process of globalization will inevitably occur. What kind of process it will be and what are the appropriate policy responses to channel it are the questions at issue.

Yet this very statement that globalization is a stage in the evolution of capitalism depends on a form of secular reasoning and presuppositions of linear change and inevitability that the Church may – will – wish to challenge. And the core of the pastoral and theological questions that such a statement evokes in an attentive Church is essentially those posed by the conduct of capitalist economies since the industrial revolution, a system that generates 'winners' and 'losers'. These are profound ethical questions. The Church cannot duck them and remain faithful to the gospel on the grounds that globalization is a complex topic, nor on the grounds that this is not altogether a purely novel context for ethics and the question has been dealt with before.

So what in this new economic context should the Church say and do about the growth in inequality that accompanies a net increase in wealth – measured as rising incomes? What should be the Church's response to an economic system that generates wealth for those able to seize opportunities but denies a living to so many and arguably endangers God's creation? Old questions in a new context that urgently demand answers. New questions about the Prometheus unbound of footloose and free capital within the shaky architecture of international finance.

economics and the Church

The Church must proclaim its own story about economics. There is no alternative. And it is at heart a simple story. Creative human action is an integral part of being human. And this pre-eminently includes work resulting in the production of goods, services for exchange, and artefacts, as well as play and the giving and receiving of gifts. Economic activity describes the harnessing of this creative action as people trying 'to make a living'. In a Christian anthropology, the way individuals and societies make a living may either embody individual self-interest in the sense of being ultimately directed towards God and the fullness of human well-being, thus being in harmony with God's purposes and providence, or sinfully reject them in selfish forms of domination with contempt for the poor and for creation.

There has yet to be found a more efficient mechanism than the market for the distribution of different goods and services, but markets are flawed. Whether or not they are seen as a providential dispensation, markets alone have not been able to, and cannot, ensure the common good through equitable distribution. A variety of institutions and interventions are necessary for this to occur. The fundamental problem with the globalization stage of capitalism is that such interventions have in the past relied on the activity of, and within, states, and the global political architecture is woefully inadequate to encompass a global economy. The policy prescriptions of the Reagan–Thatcher years systematically dismantled the ability of states to control and police the global economy. The economic has therefore dramatically outpaced the development of the political. The first demand of the Church must therefore be for urgent reform of the existing inadequate international institutions: the World Trade Organization (WTO), the International Monetary Fund (IMF) and the World Bank (WB) – in that order of urgency – to create the preconditions for a global political economy and a global social contract. The primary goal of this reform should be to ensure that the interests of the poorest countries, the 'losers', are secured. The poorest need, to use the hallowed WTO phrase, 'special and differential treatment', not as some carefully policed short-term measure, but as a response to their ongoing economic needs. The Church will find many allies in this pursuit.

Such reform demands a major challenge to the dominance of trading interests, particularly those of the United States, not least to the world's 100 leading transnational corporations whose combined assets have been calculated at some $1.8 trillion. While the movement towards a rule-based regime for trade is to be welcomed as offering some protection against the wielding of naked economic power, trade rules cannot be allowed to overrule more important priorities and the ethical imperatives of our time. Biodiversity and the integrity of creation, the 1.3 billion people living on less than $1 a day, must take precedence.

In short, the reform of the international bodies has to embody a hierarchy of values and priorities with poverty and the environment at the top. Likewise, it must strengthen governments' ability to undertake special and differential treatment of their economic problems, particularly to control different forms of foreign investment and channel it, not reduce the instruments in their hands in the name of spurious 'level playing fields'.

However, if the Church believes in a Christian understanding of what it means to be human it cannot allow the economic to be treated as a final goal. It is merely a means towards an end. The simple proclamation of this fact is good news for the poor. And the end needs stating clearly. Trade, finance and investment are instruments for the achievement of integral human development, as is economic growth itself. They are not final goals of human endeavour in themselves. They must constantly be measured against integral human development – a term that might allow a fruitful conversation with secular reason about the nature of human well-being.

For this reason the United Nations International Development Targets, the halving of world poverty by 2015, are the minimum targets of the Church and should be proclaimed and promoted as such. The Church's story needs telling in this new way for a secular world, and setting targets for the eradication of poverty reflects the centrality of the poor in the life of the Church demanded by the gospel. As Albert Nolan wrote: 'If we simply repeat the formulas of the past, our words may have the character of doctrine and dogma but they will not have the character of good news ... If our message does not take the form of good news, it is simply not the Christian gospel.'[5] This is a message no less to economists with their rigidities and orthodoxies; for much of the predicament of the poorest nations has come from rigid application of economic formulas unadapted to local circumstance and problems.

This change in the focus and language of its message will require the Church to be different internally as well as to act differently. Most immediately, the capacity of the Church to work locally, nationally and internationally needs to be better coordinated and directed at poverty eradication. Local churches and their national bodies need to facilitate the participation of the poor and their representative organizations in the formulation of national poverty strategy documents with the international financial and donor bodies, as well as making inputs themselves. At the level of leadership, lobbying of recalcitrant governments is urgent and necessary. The USA's and EU's protection of their agricultural sector is a flagrant example of how for every $1 of aid the rich nations cost the poorest $14 in lost agricultural exports.

the challenge of redistribution

The levels of inequality that resulted from the promotion of anti-poor policies on a global scale are clearly unacceptable to the Christian conscience. They create fissures in society between skilled and unskilled labour, between rural and urban, between regions, races and classes, between men and women. But shifts in the tectonic plates of the top layers of the World Bank mean that the ethical argument for equity is far from lost. Despite the sacking of the key progressive policy reformer, the chief economist Joseph Stiglitz, the 2000–2001 World Bank Report reflects a change in emphasis. 'Studies find that the responsiveness of income poverty to growth increases significantly as inequality is lowered', and 'more equal societies can actually grow faster', are key insights.[6]

So greater gender equity, and equity in general endowments and assets, has a double impact on poverty reduction because in more egalitarian societies the impact of growth rate is greater and the growth rate will itself prove to be higher. The conclusion seems to be that justice is good for the economy. The implications of this in terms of the re-establishment of redistribution as a central goal of economic management, and the reinstatement of progressive taxation as an acceptable tool of state intervention, are still far from gaining significant ground, however. On this terrain of public opinion the Church has potentially some influence. But it must practise what it preaches, particularly in the realm of gender equity and justice in the Church. Moreover what is true for national economies must *a fortiori* be true for the global economy. It is a striking and worrying feature of World Bank reports that there is virtually no mention of taxation, a key measure amongst instruments for equitable development.

Central to the Church's concerns will be the question: what is to be redistributed? Obviously income – but income is earned. Technology, skills and knowledge are the bridges to income and human development. These will enable the poor to engage more 'fairly' in labour markets. But the poor also require the institutions that will permit them to influence the market and participate more equitably in it.

Unequal access to knowledge and technology will be of particular concern to the Church. Trade-related intellectual property rights (TRIPS), safe-guarded in WTO agreements, legalize the chronic disparity between the industrialized world and the poorest nations. The latter own only 3 per cent of current patents, have minimum numbers of telephones or IT equipment, and suffer from a skills shortage in most areas of a developing economy. The preconditions for entry into the global economy do not exist. The patenting of life forms, of profound concern to agricultural communities, is clearly unacceptable to most Christians, but it is questionable whether knowledge and inventions should fall under trading rules rather than be part of coordinated plans for international development formulated in United Nations bodies.

What is being redistributed at remarkable speed in societies notable for their low levels of inequality in the past – China is a prodigious example – is a new culture of brutal competitiveness, with a startling growth in inequality and a rush for consumer goods. The economic culture of neo-liberalism on a global scale has not only heralded a new stage in capitalism but a correlated new marginalization and fragmentation of the religious. The two are connected. A distorted secular reason is spawning a distorted religious reaction. The search for global spiritual 'commodities', new age, astrology, healing cults and different forms of exclusive fundamentalism, the consumer goods of the religious marketplace, are a feature of this economic culture.

This religious disintegration is perhaps the one aspect of globalization that immediately catches the Church's attention. Yet what does the Church have to offer culturally in its own life in opposition to this dominant economic culture? The biblical themes of justice and Jubilee amount to a radical and subversive challenge, restorative and redistributive, but to what extent are they dominating the life of the Church? The debt campaign, despite the very limited debt relief agreed to date, has shown how the religious can reclaim public ground and move in from the margins where they are assigned their place. The lessons from this need to be learnt. The Church will need to draw further from its own wells in the days to come. To provide a plausible counter-culture to the culture of the global economy, it must *be* different as well as *act* differently.

chapter 2

the role of the Church in overseas development

Kevin Ward

introduction

For more than a generation now, the Churches of the North have felt a lack of confidence about their global responsibilities. There is good reason for critical self-examination about the nature of the North's religious and ideological, as well as political and economic, domination of the world. Mission has in many quarters been replaced by a concern for development, conceived as a less demanding, less oppressive, and an altogether more positive way for rich Christians of the North to relate to the poor. But the reality may well be different. Michael Taylor puts the problem very clearly:

> In fact, development programmes were in many ways just as
> disrespectful, if not more so, of other cultures and ways of seeing
> things, insisting that the North and the rich knew best. Like the
> missionaries, they were peddlers of a faith and in many cases of an
> absolutist kind of faith in a particular economic programme which they
> believed would rescue millions of people from poverty. They too went
> to the South in the guise of doing good and often ended up as the
> midwives of exploitation. And they were often less successful than the
> missionaries at recognising the rights of others to their independence
> and fostering it, trapping poor countries in new spirals of dependency,
> as the trading patterns of the world and the international debt crisis still
> show. If the fight versus poverty seemed more in tune with the spirit of
> the age (and disenchantment may now be setting in here as well), it was
> no less open to criticism and often on much the same grounds.[1]

In development, as in mission, the Churches of the North must not see themselves simply or primarily as providers. They must recognize the autonomy of the Churches of the 'Third World' to envision appropriate development. That does not mean that the Churches of the North can afford to indulge in a romanticization of the poor. The factors which constrain and warp the fair distribution of the world's resources in the

North can and do inhibit and misdirect church attempts to tackle those issues in the South too. The gospel call to promote human flourishing always involves a struggle with the sinful constitution of humanity and the structures that humans both create and in which they are trapped.

the Churches overseas and human flourishing

In many parts of the world the Christian message has been received historically as an engagement with oppressive forces: the liberation of slaves, the affirmation of marginalized groups and those under threat from political and economic forces that they can neither control nor defeat. Anti-slavery was motivated not only by British abolitionists like Wilberforce, important as he was, but by freed slaves and their descendants, for whom Christianity became a powerful means of expressing the dignity of human being. Nineteenth-century figures such as Olaudah Equiano in Britain, Bishop Samuel Crowther in West Africa, and Phillis Wheatley and Sojourner Truth in the United States were actively engaged in refashioning social and economic institutions.[2]

Notoriously, programmes for radical transformation have a whole host of unintended consequences, sometimes producing structures of greater inequality than before, creating losers as well as winners. The school, central to the Christian project in many parts of the world, has been a tool of colonialism, the chief instrument for a 'colonization of the consciousness', a Trojan horse planted to subvert local cultures from the inside, creating a class of progressive individuals unwilling passively to submit to traditional communal values.[3] But it has also been an important instrument for preserving local culture, creating opportunities for communal development.[4] The construction of a school relied on local communities to provide land, and to supply local vernacular teachers. Church and school, chapel and classroom, have often shared the same space, and in fact have often hardly been distinguished conceptually. Yet religious institutions have provided an important counterweight to the more corrosive inroads of modernity, providing cohesion to rural communities, identity and new forms of association for migrants in urban areas, the intellectual and material resources to enable societies to combat dissolution, to adapt and to survive. For Britain modernization, industrialization and economic development have been experienced as a retreat from religious values, a decline of faith. In many parts of the world the experience has been exactly the opposite: Christianity and modernization have gone hand in hand.

In India, Christianity has often appealed to low-caste or out-caste communities, for whom Christian identity became one of a repertoire of strategies to ensure rising status and a re-evaluation not only of individual status but also of the community as a whole.[5] In the African townships of Johannesburg during the era of apartheid, Christian identity was associated with values of 'respectability': economic independence, orderliness, cleanliness and fidelity in sexual relations, belief in education, hard work, abstinence from alcohol, the creation of a sphere of law and order amidst violence from both police authorities and alienated and frustrated youth gangs.[6] Revivalists like the Balokole of East Africa and more recent charismatic groups within the Church may have little direct concern for 'development' issues in any formal sense. The fact that they are 'unencumbered by large bureaucratic infra-structures and developmentalist goals' may even be an advantage.[7] Their importance often lies in their ability to give a sense of coherence and strength to the group, within a society facing economic pressure and hard-ship, in fostering an optimism about the possibility of creating a liveable environment for its members, sometimes in the face of a threatening and hostile situation, dispiriting and hopeless.

Modern Pentecostalism may sometimes seem crassly assertive and individ-ualistic, lacking in social concern. Yet the 'gospel of wealth' is not simply about tele-evangelists and conspicuous consumption, it is also about the aspirations of the poor to a better life. In Latin America, the commendable Catholic concern for the option for the poor has sometimes been perceived as too clerically directed, and unrooted (despite the importance of base communities) in the actual aspirations of the poor. The great appeal of Pentecostalism (whatever its problems as an apparent agent of American culture and global capitalism) is that it provides struggling people with an incentive to work and create a community not of hopelessness but of aspiration. It can promote a more dynamic activist form of female participation, alongside a domestication of the male, now willing to face up to responsibilities as provider and home maker.[8]

In the first years of decolonization in the mid-twentieth century, it appeared in many parts of the world that the role of the Church would increasingly be confined to the private sphere of family or voluntary grouping. The education system, often seen as embodying a foreign denominational sectarianism, was nationalized. Governments took over hospitals. Foreign business activity was now assumed by national parastatal corporations. The subsequent fail-ure of this dream of national autonomy, its collapse into misrule and authoritarianism, the failure to produce a vigorous sector of local entrepreneurs, led to the neo-liberal attack on the state in the 1980s and the imposition by the global financial institutions of structural adjustment programmes. These were intended to provide a more secure basis for economic growth even at the cost of the short-term immiseration of large sections of population. At least the illusion of autonomy was replaced by the recognition that 'Third World' societies were at the mercy of international market forces. However misdirected and inhumanly managed these programmes have turned out to be, they did provide renewed opportunity for the Churches to reclaim their traditional role in developmental issues. In some countries schools were handed back en masse to the Church authorities. Sometimes the Churches have had as little chance of succeeding as governments, handicapped by totally inadequate resources and the lack of an infrastructure. But it was hoped that they could resurrect a system of moral discipline, which had characterized the old Church systems. Despite all the difficulties, education remains a dynamic sector, with public demand for more secondary schools, and increasingly for university education. Religious institutions are finding a new sphere of developmental possibilities.

The last decade has seen a proliferation of Christian universities. Such institutions can hardly survive without external backers, and here American and international evangelical money often seems essential. The ability of the central organs of the Catholic Church to mobilize its considerable resources for educational purposes provides opportunities for local Catholic communities. Local Protestant churches (Anglican, Reformed and Methodist) feel that they are at a severe disadvantage in comparison with Catholics and many Pentecostals.[9] However, an Anglican university has been established in Uganda – The Uganda Christian University. The core traditional theological function of training clergy is supplemented by programmes in education and business studies that are remarkably popular. To pursue business studies is not simply an exercise in self-centred individualism; it can be seen as a 'rational' choice, a means of ensuring a return on the substantial capital that families (rather than individual students only) have invested at great sacrifice. From the university point of view, it helps to ensure continuing viability. Student fees will never pay for substantial capital investment in plant and textbooks. But they will help to ensure a healthy financial turnover to pay the teachers and to enable the institution to undertake its core Christian functions of ministerial training.[10]

the Churches and community development

Churches are involved in considerable developmental activity in the community: it is part of their very being rather than an extra to their 'spiritual' functions. In the churches of the Anglican Communion, Mothers' Unions often provide a most important base for developmental projects – agricultural and husbandry schemes, nutritional programmes for children, family planning, small-scale enterprises, cooperatives, credit unions, funeral support groups.[11] These activities do not depend on external funding, but naturally are often greatly invigorated by outside help. Women's groups are increasingly taking a prominent part in national affairs, utilizing skills they have learnt in local church responsibilities. In Uganda The Aids Support Organization (TASO), a non-sectarian organization supporting those living with HIV/Aids, was founded by a Catholic woman whose Protestant husband had died.[12]

The Churches are intimately involved in family planning and Aids prevention programmes, and in supporting those living with Aids, encouraging non-judgemental and supportive attitudes in the community as a whole. The Churches in Africa have often been reluctant to encourage the use of condoms as an answer to these issues, and therefore lukewarm about government campaigns, which focus on this issue. Condom use offends not only Catholic sensibilities, but also the traditional ethical teachings of most churches concerned to discourage promiscuous lifestyles and to model Christian marriage patterns. But the sheer enormity of the problem of Aids has led to increasingly flexible responses based on strong identification with human need and the necessity of strengthening traditional structures of support.

This varied activity of the Churches at local level means that they are often seen as a more reliable and potentially promising partner than formal government agencies. In fact dioceses may establish elaborate developmental projects in the hope of attracting external funding. Where they are part of a coherent programme, such projects can be of great benefit to the whole community, as well as the particular church. The strength of Protestant Churches has been that local parish life has typically been self-sufficient, dependent on local resources and enthusiasm. This can be compromised by the increasing necessity of external funding for survival.[13] Ugandans have joked about a 'theology of eating', and about the 'grabiosis' disease, in which clergy and their families are often seen as first in line for benefits, if only to compensate for the inadequacy and unpredictability of their normal remuneration.[14] Such sardonic humour is a means of coming to terms with the stark intractability of the world, unamenable to perfect solutions. It contrasts starkly with the humourless moral indignation that so easily erupts in developed economies at fairly trivial inconveniences and dysfunctions.

In a place like Pakistan, the Churches' role is necessarily more circumscribed than in most of sub-Saharan Africa. Christianity occupies a small, fragile space in an overwhelmingly Muslim society. Historically it has often attracted 'tribal' and non-caste people, equally outside both the Islamic and (pre-1947) the Hindu mainstreams. A recent study of development issues within the Church of Pakistan by Pervaiz Sultan outlines different approaches in the eight dioceses: a preoccupation with medical services in Peshawar, evangelism in Sialkot, education in Lahore (from which Raiwind and Faiselabad Dioceses were created), agricultural and rural development in Multan, tribal evangelism in Hyderabad, urban issues concerning drug addicts and the mentally handicapped in Karachi.[15] There are historical reasons as well as social, political and geographical factors for each of these emphases, and dioceses are not exclusively concerned with one issue. Sultan compares two particular visions of development which have inspired the Bishops of Multan and Hyderabad: in Multan, an 'ecumenical' concern for mobilizing marginalized and oppressed groups, whether Christian or not, to assert their rights; in Hyderabad, the influence of the evangelical 'Lausanne' concerns for a development that integrates evangelism and social uplift. Sultan notes the limitations of development programmes based on 'pre-defined theological convictions', especially when the intellectual articulation comes from outside. In reality, for most Churches there is rarely a simple alternative between evangelistic and ecumenical modes of development.

the Churches and political development

The marginal status of Christian communities like those of Pakistan contrasts with areas where Christianity provides the dominant discourse. Tim Longman's recent study of Rwanda shows how the central role of the Catholic Church in rural life meant that it became one of the chief brokers of power in the community, the provider of jobs, the arbiter of economic progress.[16] It was the particular intensity of this conflict over scarce resources that helped to ignite those class divisions that had been so hardened by the colonial experience. The perpetrators of the 1994 genocide were overwhelmingly Christian, in this most Christian of African states. The sanctuary and witness, which the Church did provide in some measure, paled into insignificance in the face of genocide. Where the Church is so central to society (as in much of sub-Saharan Africa) it tends to embody all the tensions and the conflicts of that society. But at times it gives it a strong prophetic voice. Anglican bishops like Tutu in South Africa, Gitari and Okullu in Kenya have been at the forefront in protesting against the erosion of human rights and in providing vision for a better society. The Church seems sometimes to provide the only form of political opposition or alternative government. Catholic bishops in Zaire, Cameroon and Benin have played vital roles in this process in their own countries. But by and large the actual assumption of political and governmental roles by the Church would seem to be ill-advised and unsustainable.

The urgent need in Africa is not for 'Church' direction of the 'State', but to create the conditions for good governance, in which civil society can flourish. The Christian leaders who involved themselves in the anti-apartheid movement, and who played such a central role in the protests of the 1980s, have been conscious of their need to adopt a less prominent role as South Africa has made the transition to a new, democratic, multicultural, non-racial society. But the task of facilitating affirmative action for previously disadvantaged groups (especially those which may not be popular) remains. This consideration animates Tutu's concern for gay rights within the Churches as well as the nation: 'It is highly unlikely that [Christ] will be found on the side of those who vilify and ostracise others, making them aliens, separated and cast out from the household of God.'[17] If the Church has need to examine its own exclusiveness in the light of the new society, an even more pressing question has been: how far should Christian concerns for forgiveness and reconciliation animate the society? This has been a central issue in debates about the function of the Truth and Reconciliation Commission in South Africa and what has seemed to some to be an over-emphasis on 'Christian values' in a secular, multi-religious state.[18]

the Churches and conflict resolution

Over the last decade, people in many parts of the world have had to cope not merely with the painfully slow pace of development, the failure of developmental dreams and 'expectations of modernity', but with a collapse of the structures of law and order and the ensuing endemic violence and civil war, often of a protracted, debilitating kind. In The *Mask of Anarchy* Stephen Ellis discusses the Liberian civil war, and what seems to be a collapse into barbarism and senseless cruelty, not least through the appropriation of the anti-human elements in traditional religion, freemasonry and indigenous secret societies as well as the more regressive aspects of Christianity.[19] My own experience of somewhat similar situations relates to northern Uganda, where for the past 15 years what might be seen as 'normal' society has ceased to function in a prolonged conflict between the central government and, initially, Alice Lakwena and her Holy Spirit movement, and then her uncle Joseph Kony's Lord's Resistance Army (LRA).[20]

At times these movements have been seen as totally opposed to 'development' as normally conceived. People are ordered to abandon cultivation, to move their dwellings away from the roadside and other arteries of communication with an outside world. Pastors are attacked for being agents of a central oppressive government. But the LRA has little compunction in itself inflicting vengeance – abducting boys to become soldiers and girls to become 'wives' (sex slaves). People have been mutilated and maimed in ways meant to convey symbolic messages: cutting off the arms of those participating in local (government) militias, to show that they can no longer bear arms to fight the rebels; cutting off the lips of those seen as tale bearers to government.

The Acholi people of Uganda feel that they are caught between a rock and a hard place, with the central government bearing equally hard on them, forcing them into 'protected villages' and cutting them off from their fields and cultivation. The combination of these two forces has meant a collapse in many aspects of traditional Acholi culture, in particular the obliteration of a social and moral economy based on cattle. These are times of quite appalling suffering and deprivation sustained over a long period. One of the most depressing testimonies I heard in my visit in 1999 to one of the camps in Kitgum district, eastern Acholi, was the comment that the members of the camp had been supplied weedkiller to help in the planting of crops. But people had been loath to distribute the product when they found that so many young people in despair were using the poison to try to commit suicide.[21]

Meanwhile the Churches (Catholic and Protestant) have become much more central to Acholi life. This is not an environment where Pentecostalism thrives: it does not have the independent financial resources that make possible the creation of free-standing congregations on the Pentecostal pattern. Nevertheless, even here the songs and technology and the culture associated with Pentecostalism have penetrated the Catholic and Anglican churches to which the youth who are not drawn into the direct fighting belong. Everywhere in the north the reliance on cattle is being replaced by a building boom: cows have proved too portable a currency, able to be misplaced by raiders. There is something more substantial and permanent about building houses and shops. Christians who sing that this world is not their home are also putting down foundations in this earth as never before. It is a mark of hope for the future blossoming of society.

A parallel movement has been going on in the southern Sudan, this time among the rebels against the central government in Khartoum. There the conflict has been even more long-lasting and profound than in northern Uganda. The loss of cattle, of traditional material and spiritual culture, has been compensated for by a phenomenal growth in Christianity, hardly influenced by foreign missionaries at all, but undertaken by Sudanese Christians, whose theology of suffering and the cross, expressed in hymns and in symbolic forms, has been eloquently and passionately conveyed by Marc Nikkel.[22] Here are situations where both the 'traditional' and the 'modern' have dissolved together as the institutions of power in society, both traditional elders and central organs of 'government', have withered away. Christianity is involved in the radical reorientation of a whole culture and society.

conclusion

An illuminating book on how people cope with the fragility or absence of development is *The Anthropology of Anger* by Celestin Monga, a political scientist from Cameroon.[23] The democratization movement of the early 1990s may have run out of steam, says Monga, but that does not mean that African people are not constantly struggling for ways in which to assert democratic modes of being. He talks of the importance of subversion, of 'collective insubordination', often, of necessity, indirect and hidden, of the need for people continually 'to invent in their daily lives an approach to the world that helps them give meaning to the era in which they live'. Among other things, this takes the form of irony and linguistic innovation, the street language of youth. 'This . . . allows one to conceive of other freedoms and to survive the hardships and cruelties of everyday life, the totalitarianism of political power, the theological deliriums of fundamentalists attached to a traditional culture little adapted to the times, and the yoke of the family – obsolete but still very much present.'[24] Thus reality is mocked, 'destiny' is transformed. Local Christian communities can be crucial in such development, the creative process by which people take hold of their destiny.

chapter 3

General Synod and international development

the triumph of hope over experience

Charles Reed

introduction

Responding to extreme global poverty has been a major concern for the General Synod of the Church of England. Over the last 30 years the Synod has debated various aspects of overseas development, most notably development education, fair trade, breast milk substitutes, Third World debt and the arms trade. These debates have sometimes taken place as a response to crises, such as the sub-Saharan famine of the mid-1980s. In this sense the Synod has sought to act as the nation's conscience. In so doing, the Synod has raised sharp issues and provoked fresh thought and action regarding what it is to be Church in an increasingly interdependent world.

Successive Synods have maintained that a Christian understanding of global poverty and destitution must inevitably lead to Christian action. In 1975 the Rt Revd Robert Runcie, then the Bishop of St Albans, said to the Synod:

> If we are to act effectively, we must show our concern practically, not only by personal sacrifice and personal giving through agencies such as Christian Aid, but by encouraging the Government to work for change which we believe to be right.[1]

The Synod's record on development reveals a radical agenda for global witness and action. As the campaign against Third World debt illustrates, the agenda of the twenty-first century, although more specialized than that of the 1970s, underlines the importance of Synod's, and other Church bodies', remaining engaged in international development.

fair trade, debt relief and the Jubilee vision

The widening gap between rich and poor and the perceived failure of trickle-down economics to combat global poverty has engaged the mind of the General Synod on more than one occasion. Synod has regularly emphasized the need for a 'new and more equitable system of economic relations between nations as well as the importance of working for the cancellation of official debts from severely indebted countries'.[2]

The prioritization of trade and debt relief emerged from a process of Christian reflection stimulated by a prior commitment in the 1970s and early 1980s to development education. The catalyst was a 1969 OECD report, *Partners in Development*.[3] This report proposed that, as one response to the growing gap between rich and poor nations, the industrialized nations should allocate 1 per cent of their gross national product (GNP) to aid, of which 0.7 per cent should be in official development assistance. Picking up on these themes, the 1972 Synod passed a resolution regretting the Government's decision not to accept this target.[4] In 1975 the Synod again urged the Government to raise the level of official aid to 0.7 per cent of GNP. At the same time, however, it challenged the Church to set an example by promoting an appeal to individual church members to give 1 per cent of their net take-home pay to Christian Aid and the World Development Movement.

In the 1980s successive Synods reiterated their commitment to these two points. In 1980 and again in 1986, when debating *Let Justice Flow*, Synod passed resolutions deploring the reduction in official development assistance to poorer countries and urged the Government to reverse the cuts.[5] At the same time Synod affirmed its commitment to encourage Church members to devote 1 per cent of take-home pay to development and missionary agencies in order to encourage the continued development of programmes of education in the Church on international development matters.[6] Although the establishment of 1 per cent appeals has always been patchy, it is clear that the emphasis on development education has manifested itself in the campaign for a fairer system of trade between nations as well as in the campaign for a comprehensive and one-off remission of unpayable debts.

In 1995 Synod passed a resolution urging the Government to work with the European Union in implementing affirmative policies for fair trade with the 'Third World'.[7] Synod recognized that the dumping of European agricultural surpluses onto the world market prejudiced the livelihoods of Third World farmers. Synod underlined the necessity of reforming Europe's agricultural basis, especially those subsidies provided by the European Union's Common Agricultural Policy. At the same time, Synod encouraged all congregations to sign up to Christian Aid's trade campaign by buying fairly traded products such as tea and coffee. Parishes have played a constructive role in this campaign by pressing supermarkets to buy food from those suppliers who respect labour rights and who are committed to the principles of fair trade.

Complementary to the fair trade campaign was the Jubilee 2000 Coalition against 'Third World' debt. General Synod debated this in 1991 and again in 1996. Central to Synod's vision underpinning the Jubilee 2000 Coalition was the belief that it is iniquitous to force countries to spend more money on debt repayment than on health or education. Between 1996 and 2000 the Jubilee 2000 Coalition forced Third World debt to the top of the international agenda, and in doing so it helped to bring the interest of the poorest people to the front of the economic debate. Churches were the backbone of this movement and through their extensive networks they helped to mobilize Christians and other concerned individuals up and down the country as well as further afield. According to Jubilee 2000, a staggering 24 million people around the world signed the Jubilee 2000 petition. For the many thousands who participated in the Birmingham G8 Summit demonstrations in July 1998, or the Cologne G8 demonstrations in July 1999, the sense of empowerment was exhilarating and gave renewed confidence about the value of Christian witness in a global economy. The 'bottom-up' nature of this movement was reflected at Synod by the 1996 debate on Jubilee 2000, which was prompted by a Private Member's Motion.

The Jubilee 2000 Coalition helped to secure significant debt reduction. In 1996 Jubilee 2000 campaigned for 52 countries, owing a total of $4,376 billion, to obtain debt cancellation. By December 2000, creditors had promised to cancel $110 billion of the debts of 41 countries. This is a remarkable achievement but many of the poorest countries still have to spend more on debt than on health or education. Against this background the Chancellor of the Exchequer, Gordon Brown, used a Jubilee 2000 rally on 2 December 2000 to announce that all debt payments to the UK from 41 of the world's poorest countries were to be stopped or held in trust until the day they could be returned to fund poverty reduction programmes. This was a significant announcement which it is hoped might encourage other G8 governments to take similar unilateral action.

The Church through its grass-roots networks played an influential and constructive role in campaigning for the cancellation of unpayable debt. It is important that the Church maintains and supports this momentum following the closure of the Jubilee 2000 Coalition. As part of this process Synod needs to recommit itself to the *jubilee vision* of debt relief, poverty eradication and social and economic development for the poorest communities of our world. Anne Pettifor, Director of Jubilee 2000 Coalition UK, said:

> One of the most profound lessons from the Jubilee 2000 campaign is this, we will not get more debt cancellation until we have changed the process whereby debt cancellation is agreed. The next campaign, therefore, has to tackle the deep structural injustices of international financial relationships.[8]

Christian Aid's new campaign on trade should provide the Church of England and its ecumenical partners with a valuable opportunity to realize this vision by advocating a more equitable trading system which works to the advantage rather than the detriment of the world's poorest nations.

The emphasis on trade reflects a wider concern with that phenomenon commonly called 'globalization'. In December 1998 *Faith in a Global Economy*, a report published by the Church of England's Board for Social Responsibility, addressed the challenge of poverty in a global economy.[9] Intended as a contribution to a worldwide challenge, the report rejected a narrowly economic understanding of how society works and what motivates people. Mirroring the theology of previous Synod debates, the report stated:

> Much more is at stake than whether people have enough food to stop them starving. People cannot live 'by bread alone'. We believe that there is a need for much deeper reflection on what it means to be human, how these insights inform our views of what a humane society is, and how we develop an economy which exists for people – rather than providing for them as consumers or discarding them as redundant if there are not enough jobs to go round.[10]

The recognition that everybody is a moral subject has shaped Synod's engagement with world poverty and its underlying causes, such as conflict.

the arms trade

A major cause of poverty in many parts of the world has been the prevalence and persistence of armed conflict. It is evident that in some 100 developing countries there is a relationship between domestic and regional conflicts and the spread of poverty and stagnation or decline. The 1994 Human Development Report calculated, for instance, that: 'In poor countries the chances of dying from malnutrition or preventable disease are 33 times greater than the chances of dying in a war with the neighbours. Yet on average, poor countries have about 20 soldiers for every doctor.'[11] Twenty of the world's 34 poorest countries are either in conflict or are just emerging from conflict. The persistence of conflict is a major prohibitive factor in the debt relief process. Indeed, the World Bank has indicated that ten of the most heavily indebted poor countries are unable to qualify for debt relief because of their involvement in conflict.[12]

Although there is a long-established tradition of pacifism within Christianity, the Church as a whole has never condemned all wars or the use of force. The Church's most recent thinking on the issue, contained in the Board for Social Responsibility report *Responsibility in Arms Transfer Policy*, emphasized that the right to self-defence as recognized in Article 51 of the United Nations Charter is just and necessary.[13] This means that those countries that are not arms producers must be able to acquire the means of self-defence. Unless one is a pacifist, rejecting both the use of violence as well as the provision of the instruments of violence, the pivotal issue becomes that of the criteria by which arms transfer ought to be restricted or allowed. This question is all the more important given the obvious implications that an irresponsible arms transfer policy might have for international development.

Synod maintains that Britain, as the second largest exporter of arms, has a special responsibility to ensure that its arms exports are not used for unethical purposes. The 1994 Synod, meeting in the aftermath of the arms to Iraq affair, held that any arms transfer policy should be ethically responsible, transparent, publicly accountable and consistent. It called for: (1) subordination of commercial criteria to political and ethical judgement; (2) clear separation between arms transfers and provision of aid; (3) refusal of arms transfers to countries engaged in, or likely to engage in, aggression; (4) refusal of arms to regions of tension; (5) removal of direct and indirect government subsidies for arms transfers; (6) rejection of arms transfers to countries guilty of grave and consistent patterns of human rights violations;

(7) rejection of arms transfers to countries in breach of international law; (8) support for an international ban on the production and transfer of anti-personnel mines, including prohibition of their export from the United Kingdom; and (9) the development of a coordinated policy with European Union partners, in order to ensure that the boundaries of the single European Market are effectively controlled to agreed high standards with regard to export of arms and dual use equipment.[14]

Many of the points listed above are now reflected in government policy, as shown by the European Code of Conduct on Arms Transfer Policy, but it is clear that further progress is needed. The Government's decision to issue seven licences for the sale of Hawk aircraft spares to Zimbabwe in February 2000 appeared to contravene both the UK and EU codes of conduct. The Church must remain engaged in this area since the arms trade remains a litmus test of the Government's commitment to inject an ethical dimension into foreign policy. A recent report by the House of Commons International Development Committee concluded that:

> The lack of proportion between the expenditure of developing countries on arms and their expenditure on social sectors is a scandal, and one in which many developed arms-exporting countries are implicated. The United Kingdom is of course the second largest exporter of arms in the world. The Government must, as a priority, ensure coherence across all departments so that its policy is credible. Other policies must not conflict with development policy.[15]

In this respect it is disappointing that, even after four years, the Government has still not acted upon the recommendations made in the 1996 Scott Report. Current export control legislation remains fundamentally unchanged since 1939.

If the Church expects Government coherence on arms-related matters then it must show some coherence in its own policy. In this respect, armaments, defence and the international trade in arms have been among the most complex and controversial issues for the Church of England's investment bodies, where the line between fiduciary duty and ethical expectation is at its sharpest.[16] The Church, through its central investment bodies the Church Commissioners, the CBF Church of England Funds and the Church of England Pensions Board, has long had a policy of avoiding investment in companies that supply armaments. The evolving nature of conflict, however, together with changes in the arms industry and in the system of national and international regulation, suggested that it was time to review the Church's policy to ensure that it continues to be valid.

A review conducted by the Ethical Investment Advisory Group (EIAG), of which the Board for Social Responsibility is a member, recommended to the three central investment institutions that henceforth investment should be avoided completely in manufacturers of military platforms such as aircraft, ships, tanks, helicopters and armoured vehicles, as well as suppliers of weapons and weapons systems. Investment in suppliers of non-offensive equipment such as avionic systems, instrumentation and components would be acceptable where this constituted less than 25 per cent of revenue. Companies with defence turnover in the range 20–25 per cent would be closely monitored and reviewed by investment managers and the EIAG. The three investment bodies subsequently endorsed these recommendations. In reaching its conclusions the EIAG determined that a policy combining product and volume focus would have a positive effect as it removes the Church from the taint of complicity in the sale of platforms and offensive equipment to countries with dubious human rights records, thereby meeting ethical investment expectations. In turn it found that adopting these criteria would have only a marginal effect on fiduciary duty. This review resulted in the decision to withdraw the Church's investment in the company GKN.

the promotion of breast milk substitutes

During the 1990s Synod debated on three occasions issues surrounding the promotion of breast milk substitutes. The matter was considered of vital importance, affecting as it does the health and indeed survival of some of the world's most vulnerable infants. These debates with their heavy emphasis on a specific development issue reflected Synod's willingness to engage in a sophisticated campaign for social justice. Yet whereas the Jubilee 2000 Coalition showed what was possible through social action, the campaign against breast milk substitutes illustrated its constraints.

In July 1991 a debate in General Synod on the free promotion of breast milk substitutes in the Third World led to a successful motion endorsing 'the call to stop purchasing Nescafé'. The Synod suspended this boycott in July 1994 on the evidence provided by UNICEF and the World Health Organization (WHO) that only two developing countries were without agreements or laws to end the free subsidized supplies of breast milk substitutes in Third World hospitals and maternity wards. This decision was taken, however, on the understanding that the decision to suspend the boycott would be reconsidered if Nestlé failed to comply with the World Health Assembly Resolution of May 1994. In July 1997 General Synod once again debated the issue. The Synod stressed the need to promote infant and maternal health by all available means when it passed a motion endorsing the conclusions of the report *Cracking the Code*, which was produced by the Interagency Group on Breast-feeding Monitoring (IGBM).[17]

The IGBM is a coalition of almost 30 non-governmental organizations, including development agencies and Church bodies such as the Board for Social Responsibility. The coalition was formed in order to conduct research into companies' compliance with the International Code of Marketing of Breast-milk Substitutes. The main conclusion of *Cracking the Code*, which reflected research conducted in Poland, Bangladesh, Thailand and South Africa, was that major manufacturers of breast milk substitutes continued to contravene the international code of marketing of breast milk substitutes, thereby jeopardizing the lives of infants. Violations highlighted by the report included the donation of free breast milk substitute samples, the publication of printed materials that undermined breastfeeding, and unsolicited visits by company representatives to health facilities.

It is through the IGBM and its attempts at dialogue with the infant formula industry that the Board for Social Responsibility has attempted to follow up on decisions taken by General Synod. The effectiveness of this dialogue has always been impaired by the inability of the infant formula industry and the IGBM to agree common terms of reference. Nestlé questioned not only the conclusions of *Cracking the Code* but also the methodological framework that supported the conclusions. Since the report was conducted on a very small budget and within a very short timescale, and since the IGBM had nothing like the resources of the International Association of Infant Food Manufacturers behind it, the report was easy to dismiss. *Promotion of Breast-milk Substitutes*, prepared by the Board for Social Responsibility for the 1997 General Synod, stated that 'the round of charge and counter-charge relating to basic facts, to their interpretation and the good faith of the various parties appears to be endless'.[18] It is worth noting that in the run-up to the General Synod proceedings at York in 1997 Nestlé vigorously lobbied General Synod members by handing out leaflets urging people to vote in a certain way. Many Synod members complained that such activities gave the feeling that the Synod was being unduly pressurized.

The Board for Social Responsibility continues to be an active partner of the IGBM. The IGBM is currently drawing up a new research project aimed at determining to what extent companies comply with the International Code of Marketing of Breast-milk Substitutes and subsequent World Health Assembly Resolutions. This work is important because the code is still being violated in many countries and companies show little commitment to its provisions. In 1998 the *British Medical Journal* reported that there was compelling evidence to suggest that the code was being widely violated.[19] This means that infant lives are threatened and the mother's right to an informed choice over how to feed her baby is jeopardized. The poorest mothers are those who suffer most from this reality.

As well as through the IGBM, the Church of England maintains a critical dialogue with Nestlé through EIAG. In what remains a very polarized debate EIAG acts as an interlocutor for the Church in referring any alleged breaches of the WHO code to the companies concerned for comment. Despite the obvious charge of complicity, it is clear that the contentious and controversial nature of breast milk substitutes makes such a dialogue both desirable and necessary. The WHO estimates that 1.5 million deaths a year could be prevented by effective breastfeeding protection.

conclusion

Central to recent debates about globalization is the question of how it can be made to work for the benefit of the world's poor. There are currently over 1.3 billion people living in absolute poverty. This is clearly an unacceptable situation. The response of the international community to the growing economic and social disparity has been to set the target of halving world poverty by 2015. To achieve this aim, the international community has agreed various subsidiary targets, which include universal primary education, basic health care for all and environmental and health targets that require the provision of clean water and sanitation. In November 1998 Clare Short, the Secretary of State for International Development, addressed General Synod on the contribution that the Church of England could make to combat poverty. At the end of her speech she challenged the Church to 'construct a worldwide alliance of people of faith and moral purpose to ensure that we commit ourselves to the elimination of extreme poverty from the world during the next century'.[20]

The record presented here illustrates that Synod recognizes the need to combat poverty. In 1981, during the debate on the Brandt Report, the Rt

Revd Cyril Bowles, then Bishop of Derby, said, 'The Synod must use the language of Christian theology in calling the people of our churches, the people of our nation, and all people at present alive on this planet, to repentance for such appalling global poverty.'[21] An understanding that one in four people today live on less than $1 per day suggests that little has changed internationally. According to the World Bank's World Development Report 2000–2001, the average income in the richest 20 countries is 37 times the average in the poorest 20 – a gap that has doubled in the past 40 years.[22] Re-reading past synodical debates on international development it is possible to discern a theology which recognizes that somewhere in the whole nexus of causes of global poverty our choices and decisions have contributed to the situations that justify such comparisons. Although it is encouraging that the Government is soliciting the support of the Churches, it is important that Synod does not lose sight of this theology, which underpins its understanding of global poverty and which in turn determines its social action.

part II
the challenge of globalization

chapter 4

the UK's aid programme

John Montagu

political background

When New Labour came to power in 1997 there was tremendous expectation
among the aid agencies, including Christian Aid and CAFOD, which was
reflected in their submissions to the 1997 White Paper *Eliminating World
Poverty*.[1] Many of the new ideas in that statement came from the agencies
themselves, whose staff, after years of lobbying, were for the first time
engaging closely with departmental officials; in some cases they had even
become those officials. To be fair, this process had begun in the early
1990s under the previous aid administration. Consultation and transparency were the new order of the day, and there was genuine common
ground on the best way forward for developing countries in aid and debt
relief, if not in trade and foreign policy.

Under the 1997 White Paper both the quality and the quantity of aid were
due to improve, with a new emphasis on poverty reduction according to
the new International Development Targets. Most of these targets, based on
1990 statistics, were set at the UN summits at Copenhagen and Beijing in
1995 and are monitored by the World Bank and the OECD's Development
Assistance Committee. They include a commitment to halve the proportion
of the world's population living on less than $1 a day (calculated at 23 per
cent, or 1.3 billion people, in 1995) by 2015.

The task of transforming official aid policies, even under energetic leadership, is Herculean. Inevitably, after three years (by the end of 2000) there
has been some disappointment with the Government's progress. Taking aid
alone, the forecasts for 2000–01, while beginning to reverse the downward
trend under the Conservative Government to below 0.3 per cent of gross
national product (GNP), have still failed to get any nearer to the long-
established UN target of 0.7 per cent. The planned increase to £3.6 billion
in 2003–4, which has been welcomed, still only brings aid up to 0.33 per
cent of GNP.

No one could disagree with the international targets as objectives, but
independent evaluations of progress towards targets to date are random
and have shown no significant advances against poverty in international

terms. Sustainable development, a fine objective, is hard to measure. Debt relief has been a popular platform but even in the Chancellor's initiatives at the Birmingham and Cologne G7 summits there was a discrepancy between the announced 100 per cent relief and the sums actually transmitted, let alone evidence of measurable gains in poverty alleviation in the indebted countries.

Overall, changes in aid policy have been slow to percolate through the system. The much-heralded end of the Aid and Trade Provision, which had enabled UK companies to win contracts for giant power projects like the Pergau Dam, did not result in any immediate culture change at the Department of Trade and Industry (DTI). The Export Credits Guarantee Department has survived an exhaustive mission and status review, and new international controls on the arms trade are only beginning to influence the political climate. Efforts towards 'joined-up' government and collaboration between departments both at home and in the European Union have made an impact on the civil service, but not yet on overseas programmes. In short, the Government has overreached itself: it has set itself a tremendous and laudable task but has not convinced anyone it can complete it.

implementing new policies

Despite these frustrations and delays, the achievements of the 1997 White Paper, and its successor, *Eliminating World Poverty: Making Globalisation Work for the Poor*, promise to be considerable.[2] The overall objectives and strategy of the Department for International Development (DfID) have indicated exciting new directions. Globalization, which is already setting some of the agenda for foreign policy, brings aid further into the mainstream of trade and development. Sustainable development, good governance, human rights, transparency, the control of corruption, the strengthening of civil society and capacity building are part of the new humanitarian vocabulary of aid that now belongs to the IMF and the World Bank too: the new aid conditionality linked to poverty reduction strategies. The harsh language of structural adjustment, the stick used by the IMF, has given way to the deceptively soothing tones of debt relief and poverty alleviation.

There is considerable public support in the UK for the development targets and in a few countries there has been notable progress. The World Bank reported a fall from 420 million poor in East Asia in 1987 to 280 million in 1998. Figures provided to the UN General Assembly last June showed that the proportion of people living in extreme poverty declined in 1995–2000 from 28 per cent to 24 per cent. However, these figures disguise huge regional imbalances such as, for example, a degree of poverty reduction in China. Meanwhile the absolute number of people in poverty rose during that period, both because of population increases, especially in sub-Saharan Africa and South Asia, and because of growing poverty in areas such as the former Soviet Union. The number of people living on less than $1 a day is still 1.2 billion. The gap between rich and poor is widening, with the average income in the 20 richest countries now 37 times the average in the poorest 20.

The development targets are now beginning to look unrealistic, given that only one-third to a half of the countries concerned had accepted them by 2000. Out of 140 states surveyed by the United Nations Development Programme since 1998, only 43 had poverty reduction plans or had set targets to eradicate poverty. Work by the Overseas Development Institute shows that few African countries are likely to reach the targets. A 1998 Christian Aid study of Uganda shows that only the education targets are likely to be met, and this is in a country which fulfils most of the necessary conditions for aid.

Some agencies, such as Christian Aid and CAFOD, believe it would be safer for the British government to concentrate on the intermediate five-year targets that are being set in individual countries rather than to mislead the public with unrealizable international targets. It is argued that some governments are not interested in poverty reduction. The targets most likely to succeed are those that command political will at the highest level in the poorest countries, and where progress has already been measured, for example in universal primary education.

There are no agreed international guidelines for implementing the development targets, and methods of evaluation vary from country to country, depending on the strength of the statistical base. Poverty eradication plans, identified by the World Bank's Poverty Reduction Strategy Papers (PRSPs), depend on other factors, such as the 100 per cent cancellation of the unpayable debts of the highly indebted countries (assuming they qualify under the HIPC (heavily indebted poor countries) rules). Other factors of importance include 'good governance', the strengthening of civil society (which includes the non-government agencies and churches), the full participation of local people in development and the involvement of women in political and economic decision-making. In some countries, non-governmental organizations (NGOs) and Churches are involved in the implementation of PRSPs as well as in the projects themselves.

There has been a welcome new emphasis on monitoring and evaluation in all areas of government aid policy. However, it is not easy to achieve an international standard of evaluation or to compare the UK's performance with that of other donors over a wide range of countries and sectors. DfID's Departmental Report for 2000 revealed some discrepancies between the evaluations of progress towards targets in each of the 30 developing countries selected and those of the internal performance of the department itself, which have to follow stricter criteria.

new aid strategies

On the ground, in the poorest countries, it is even harder to match the neat methodology beloved of aid experts and civil servants in the North. In the attempt to apply international criteria in favoured countries like Uganda, Mozambique, Bangladesh and some Indian states which meet the new conditions, the IMF and the World Bank have embarked on joint strategies to implement the PRSPs and gradually replace or disguise the harsher process of structural adjustment.

At the same time there has been a deliberate shift back from project aid to sectoral programme aid. Rather like the denominational missions, the old, self-contained 'integrated rural development' projects, which once enjoyed a degree of self-rule, are out of favour. In some regions such as East Africa the UK and other donors have moved towards direct budgetary support for agreed objectives, enabling governments to implement programmes themselves. In 'post-conflict' and heavily indebted poor countries (HIPCs) like Uganda and Rwanda, major 'Paris Club' donors like DfID are now much more closely involved alongside the IMF and the Bank in regular dialogue with the government. In these countries issues of basic human development such as health and family planning, education, agriculture and rural credit are now tested against a range of new global priorities. These priorities are linked to international trade and foreign policy objectives such as fair trade, core labour and environmental standards, human rights, conflict prevention, legal aid and corporate responsibility. The emphasis everywhere is as much on capacity building, the strengthening of institutions or the development of markets – the future guarantees of sustainability – as it is on the implementation of the projects themselves.

Sometimes, as DfID country papers and evaluations show, the rhetoric of policy can mask the practical benefits. Rebuilding houses and businesses after a war or a storm is one thing, but true 'sustainable development' varies in character and is almost impossible to measure according to standards set in Whitehall or Brussels. The long-term success of a school or a clinic may nowadays be derived from a local enterprise such as a poultry farm or a maize flour mill rather than from state support only. Privatization has introduced business techniques into traditional development projects. Some projects have successfully broken the mould, combining old ways with new ones. Women, for example, have been more involved in income generation, project management and entrepreneurial training. More funding has gone into micro-credit and small-scale enterprises and loan schemes. There has been some successful experimental funding – Grameen Bank lending to small rural enterprises in Bangladesh, for example, or micro-health insurance for Aids victims in Uganda.

Some of these hybrid projects are funded through international NGOs. In some instances, however, DfID has been able to bypass the international NGOs in countries like India and Nepal where it has a substantial presence, and work directly with local NGOs. Meanwhile, agencies like Christian Aid, Action Aid and CAFOD are working more closely with selected 'partner' NGOs who work in turn alongside community-based organizations and increasingly take part in international campaigns, for example against child labour. In the UK, education, lobbying and campaigning within the parameters of charity law have sharpened the public image of overseas aid. DfID's new Partnership Programme Agreements with the larger international NGOs like Christian Aid and Oxfam have provided more stability in project planning, while its Civil Society Challenge Fund has deliberately strengthened links between government and the smaller NGOs and trade unions which until now have had less of the limelight. Improved fund-raising and Lottery funding has also enabled smaller, more specialized NGOs to get off the ground.

the quality of aid

A report by Christian Aid in 1998 examined the quality and effectiveness of the UK development programme in Mozambique and India. The report was highly critical of the imbalance between different channels of aid. DfID, having made a major commitment to the people of Mozambique, has strengthened its staff in Maputo so as to work through a variety of official and NGO channels. However, it will not have the capacity to achieve its stated aim, an improvement in the education and health of the poor, while remaining a key player at the level of major government services like Customs and Excise. The temptation, because of the UK's ability to supply skilled personnel and high technology, will always be to remain in the important sectors of transport and public services and encourage private investment along the Maputo corridor to South Africa.

This will always be a classic dilemma for a government aid programme which is constantly promising poverty reduction and pro-poor grass-roots develop-ment to UK taxpayers, while its partnership with other donors and governments often demands a return to infrastructural programme aid at a much higher level. The justification for this, of course, is that by working at both ends of the spectrum it will be possible to reach an appropriate level of development. The reality is that it may find itself so stretched that it achieves little in national terms except for measurable but isolated private sector or NGO projects. At the same time bilateral aid from the UK must take account of aid from other donors, which may be competitive rather than complementary.

DfID has similar problems in poor regions of countries like India where one would expect there to be more highly developed infrastructure and local services. The UK is still among India's major aid donors, third in line after Japan and Germany, and the largest contributor of grant aid. While most foreign aid is still allocated to energy and communications, including infor-mation technology, the UK's former Overseas Development Administration (ODA) made a conscious effort to move away from large energy projects towards social services. Unfortunately, the same cycle occurred. The more it concentrated on people-based development, the more difficulty it had in strengthening local capacity and meeting people's needs. In fact, a lot of UK aid has been usefully spent on proper evaluation and assessment of the mistakes made and the lessons learned. Not for the first time, the neces-sity for us to learn what the poor need and how we can help has almost outweighed the actual benefit to the people.

Only after 15 years was it fully appreciated that two major projects in India – the Orissa Health and Family Welfare Project and the Andhra Pradesh Primary Education Project – had relied too heavily on the local health and education authorities and not enough on the communities themselves.

While the statistics of thousands of trained health workers and teachers were impressive, buildings were put up that were inadequately designed and located and so not properly used. The DfID has to its credit recognized the problems and have already remodelled both these projects with some involvement from NGOs.

But the question remains unanswered: how can an outside government support sustainable projects in remote rural areas without either creating its own imported models or depending too much on inadequate local government and unaccountable NGOs? 'Civil society', the fashionable new term for participatory development, often disguises the true pattern of unequal, unrepresentative and even corrupt local democracy which is always ready to pick up spare aid money. In areas of conflict or anarchy, such as parts of the former Soviet Union, identifying genuinely sustainable development or effective NGO partners has been a challenge for DfID, the EU and aid agencies alike.

reaching the poorest

There are many areas of the world in which the poorest do not even belong to a unified state and are, as a result, out of reach of any government aid. While Sierra Leone may be seen as an illustration of Britain's ethical foreign policy at its best, the example of Sudan shows the failure of its 'enlightened' development policy. The civil war has left the people of the southern Sudan living on airlifts or food handouts, largely cut off from the world of development aid, with few prospects of change, and the country's infrastructure and institutions in ruins. Here is a powerful case for a new diplomatic and aid initiative, but so far the British government, despite its stated commitment and traditional links, has been unwilling to find a means of delivering development aid even through British NGOs, which are active in some of the more peaceful areas of the south.

A similar aid vacuum exists in the Eastern Democratic Republic of Congo, and there are others in Iraqi Kurdistan, Armenia, Tibet and Afghanistan. Huge religious and ethnic minorities exist within states in many parts of the world. More often than not these communities exist inside boundaries arbitrarily drawn up by the colonial powers, and yet those powers have had neither the will, nor the capacity, to gain access to them. These experiences are in sharp contrast to what has been achieved in Bosnia and Kosovo.

conflict and emergencies

When it comes to conflict and emergencies Britain has, in fact, had a high profile within the United Nations agencies both in terms of funding level and performance. Unlike the United States it has kept up its payments to UNHCR, UNICEF and the newer humanitarian agencies like the Human Rights Commission. DfID has been active for many years in refugee work in countries like Thailand and Sudan, supporting sensitive work by NGOs, Churches and the UN. Sometimes, as in the Great Lakes region, it is hard to balance this work against other foreign policy objectives when ethnic groups use asylum as a means of recovery and retaliation.

DfID has expanded this work considerably through its Conflict and Humanitarian Affairs Department. Working closely with recognized human rights NGOs it has developed a new reconciliation role in some post-conflict countries, strengthening the judicial process, negotiating and applying UN conventions, encouraging conflict resolution and attempting to pursue war criminals through the international courts. In other countries, like Iraq, strategic concerns have prevented humanitarian work altogether.

the EU aid programme

Relations between Britain and Europe over development aid, never healthy, reached a new low at the end of the 1990s when the entire European Commission under Jacques Santer was forced to resign, accused of allowing excessive bureaucracy, irregularities and even fraud in various directorates. The EU's external assistance programme, to which the UK is contributing about £720 million in 2000–01, one-quarter of the total DfID budget, came in for particular criticism for its slow and cumbersome procedures which have harmed poor countries as well as the aid agencies or NGOs that have been its partners or recipients.

As a result, the new Commissioners, Poul Nielson and Chris Patten, have had to carry out widespread reforms in the management of the European Development Fund and the EC Humanitarian Office (ECHO). In August 2000 the House of Commons International Development Committee complained that these reforms had still not been fully implemented, and in October the Government was forced to agree that too little had been done. As part of a wide redeployment of posts, 400 new posts have been approved to help allocate funds and manage programmes all over the world. Inevitably the internal reform process and the need for extra financial safeguards has meant further delays in implementation.

The EU has been criticized for failing to focus adequately on poverty reduction. The proportion of development assistance directed to low-income countries fell from 75 per cent in 1987 to 51 per cent ten years later, largely because of new priorities in eastern Europe and the former Soviet Union, including 'pre-accession' funding to countries joining the EU. Spending per head in 1996 had reached $4.50 in those countries, compared to only $0.7 in low-income countries. However, largely thanks to pressure from Britain, the Commission has recently made a declaration which contains a new commitment to poverty reduction and a sharper focus in the targeting of its programmes. However, this will only apply to some regions, and it will take several years to have any impact on the poorest countries.

a new trade policy

Since the 1999 World Trade Organization (WTO) Ministerial in Seattle the Government, while reasserting its free trade policy, has shown a positive attitude to critics of the new World Trade Organization and recognizes the necessity for the adoption of core labour and environmental standards in trade, whether through the WTO or the International Labour Organization (ILO). It has helped to foster the ethical trading initiative started by the NGOs and has presided over a new era of fair trade spearheaded by a few importing companies acting through the Fair Trade Foundation and now boasted by several supermarkets. It has at the same time encouraged the implementation of a human rights element in trade policy, the new international labour laws and, where possible, legislation to regulate direct and indirect exports of weapons and technology incompatible with development policy.

The Ilisu Dam project in eastern Turkey, which was investigated by the International Development Committee, became a focal point of interdepartmental controversy when the new environmental guidelines being followed somewhat reluctantly by the DTI – in this case, to protect thousands of displaced Kurdish villagers in the path of a dam being built partly by a British construction company – breached the Government's long-established trade practice.

One result of this attempted change of direction has been the review of the Export Credits Guarantee Department (ECGD), presented to Parliament in July 2000 by the DTI. Restating the principal objective of trade policy as the encouragement of British trade and investment overseas, the review accepts the inevitability of matching its activities with 'other government objectives, including those on sustainable development, human rights, good governance and trade'.[3] It remains to be seen how far this works out in practice, but it will coincide with the fashion for corporate responsibility, which is currently sweeping through the larger multinationals. Getting round the new rules will become as much a game for exporters as tax avoidance, but with fewer sanctions. For a start, many other countries do not have any guidelines. The UK government still has to convince other OECD members that the whole exercise, like so many other ethical policies, is not only right in itself, but also internationally workable. A similar situation prevails in the implementation of the Kyoto rules on climatic change, which will also have an impact on trade policy.

conclusion

The Churches and NGOs may feel some satisfaction with the effect of their campaigns on fairer trade, debt and aid, now that the British government is taking up many of their ideas. Yet it will be hard for the Government to engage on every front or associate itself too closely with NGOs and civil society, partly because of the huge demands placed upon it and the inadequacy of its resources. The International Development Targets are still elusive in spite of a new drive towards regular evaluation in the countries concerned and an attempt to use debt relief to find the appropriate poverty reduction strategies. In the developing world, local under-capacity and the constant pressure to find well-balanced projects contrast with the desperate need for investment in infrastructure and the technical skills that the UK has to offer.

In many ways this Government's success will depend on the willingness of other major donors. It is fair to say, however, that a decisive move has been made to contribute new resources to achieve a fairer world, to identify the advantages of globalization, and to meet the needs of the poorest – especially those that people express themselves rather than those introduced from outside.

chapter 5
HIV/Aids

a window on development

Gillian Paterson

A decade ago, HIV/AIDS was regarded primarily as a serious health crisis. Estimates in 1991 predicted that in sub-Saharan Africa, by the end of the decade, 9 million people would be infected and 5 million would die – a threefold underestimation. Today it is clear that AIDS is a development crisis, and in some parts of the world is rapidly becoming a security crisis too. There is now compelling evidence that the trend in HIV infection will have a profound effect on maternal mortality, life expectancy and economic growth. These unprecedented impacts at the macro-level are matched by the intense burden of suffering among individuals and households. AIDS is unique in its devastating impact on the social, economic and demographic underpinnings of development.[1]

Harriet's story

Kassinga shanty compound is an area of 'unofficial' housing on the edge of Lusaka, Zambia.[2] The red-earth streets are full of children, dogs, and the occasional chicken. Not much grows in Kassinga, and when you collect water from the communal pump, you pay 100 kwacha for the privilege. Harriet lives in a dark room round the back of a derelict-looking house, with four children of her own and Kenny, her grandchild, who is three.

Harriet is HIV positive, sputum tests indicate that she has tuberculosis, and she has many other health problems as well. Her husband, who was a truck driver, died of Aids a year ago, followed by her eldest daughter (Kenny's mother). Now her 19-year-old son Joel is sick, and huddled under the cover on the only bed. He has been out looking for work, though most of the time he is not really fit enough to work, and now he is tired and hungry. There is no food in the house. Harriet used to sell eggs till a couple of months ago, but then she had to spend the egg money on the rent. She has never been able to get going again. Honestly, she can't see that she ever will, with the triple burden of rent, sickness and the family. There are always ways, of course, for women to earn money, and rather than see her children starve . . . But these days, she is so tired . . .

Yesterday she went to the hospital. In order to qualify for drug treatments and emergency food supplies, she needs an official certificate saying she has TB. She borrowed the money to get there from a neighbour. On arrival, she found that the doctor was not there, and that there was no TB medicine in the hospital pharmacy. 'Come back next week,' she was told. But would she? Yes, maybe. If she could get the money. But people she met said this was the third week running there was no medicine. The private pharmacies had stocks, but who could afford to go there? So maybe it was easier just to let the disease take its course.

how did she become infected with HIV?

How does anybody? She has never played away from home herself, but she always assumed her husband had other women when he was away, after all a man needs to have sex regularly. And no, she would never have thought of asking him to use a condom. 'In my culture,' she says, 'we have to have babies, and if we do not have them our husbands take other wives. He would have been shocked if he thought I knew about the condom. That's how it is with us,' she says, and laughs for the first time.

Where are the other children, I ask. Her own youngest, a boy, is at school, paid for by an uncle, but there is no school on the shanty compound, and he has to walk 6 miles a day to get there. The two girls are out somewhere. They are good girls, but there is no money for books and uniforms and all the things you need to send them to school. Her parents live back in the village, and they are looking after the children of two other brothers who have died. 'I will die too,' says Harriet. 'My biggest worry is, what will happen to my children and my grandson? Kenny and the girls will have to go to my parents, but they are old and poor, and they are already looking after eight grandchildren . . .'

Gertrude, her friend, appears in the doorway and stands there quietly. 'Come with me,' says Harriet and we get up to go out. It is a relief to escape. It is not just the darkness and the confined space and the silent boy on the bed that make it claustrophobic, it is the hopelessness of it all. Outside, it is clean and cold in the winter sunshine, and five or six women are sitting on the ground, chatting idly and brushing flies off a young girl who is lying on the ground, vacant-eyed and without the strength to move. Harriet's whole face brightens as she greets her friends. It is time for the meeting of the local widows' group, supported by a non-governmental organization (NGO) called CINDI (Children in Distress).

what will kill Harriet?

Harriet will die within the next couple of years, and so probably will Joel.
The children will become orphans. Back in the village, her elderly parents
will be left looking after ten or eleven grandchildren and one great-grandchild.

In the developing world, HIV is mainly transmitted via heterosexual inter-
course with an infected partner. In 1999, 2.8 million people died of Aids,
of whom 1.2 million were women, and half a million were children under the
age of fifteen. Worldwide, since the beginning of the epidemic, 13.2 million
children have been orphaned.[3] In 1998, HIV prevalence among women
between the ages of 20 and 24 was estimated at 30 per cent in Mutasa
District, Zimbabwe (a rural area), and a horrifying 58 per cent in
Carletonville, South Africa. In Africa in general, for every 10 men infected
with HIV there are 12 or 13 women.[4]

Table 5.1 Adults and children living with HIV/Aids, January 2000

Sub-Saharan Africa	24.5 million
South and South-East Asia	5.6 million
Latin America	1.3 million
North America	0.9 million
East Asia and Pacific	0.53 million
Western Europe	0.52 million
Eastern Europe and Central Asia	0.42 million
Caribbean	0.36 million
North Africa and Middle East	0.22 million

Aids is caused by infection with HIV, but the huge majority of people living
with HIV/Aids are in the poorest countries, and the link between HIV and
poverty is now accepted by all responsible authorities. HIV transmission
rates are exacerbated by poverty. Crumbling health services that are
inaccessible to the poor may lead to increased risk of infection as other
sexually transmitted illnesses (STIs) are ignored. Opportunistic infections
associated with AIDS may go untreated because of the cost or unavailability
of drugs. Young people with no work and no education are particularly
vulnerable to temptation, and with no prospect of a better life in the future,
there is little incentive to avoid risky behaviour. In June 2000, UNAIDS
projected that Aids would eventually kill half of all Ethiopian and South
African boys who were then aged 15.

HIV and its associated illnesses lead to poverty, too, because they occur mainly in young parents and breadwinners. Aids is a long, debilitating process that stops people working. The burden of caring is costly for families and communities, access to health care is often limited, and even the most basic treatments may have to be paid for. The next generation loses out on education, as school fees become increasingly unaffordable. Meanwhile, orphans and elderly grandparents may be left without income, and national resources drained by the burden of caring for so many sick.

Poverty plays an absolutely crucial role in fuelling the HIV epidemic. However, it is only one element in the cocktail of deprivation. HIV becomes a window on the development process by spotlighting marginalization, poverty, violence, the oppression of women and the exclusion of minorities.

First, experience with HIV/Aids endorses the central place of women's rights within the development agenda. 'The empowerment of women' is sometimes presented as a rich-world luxury that the poor cannot afford, but if women are totally dependent economically on men, if they do not have enforceable rights to property, if they have no power to regulate the circumstances of their sexual encounters, then they become a danger not just to themselves but to the whole community. As a (male) village leader in Uganda said to me, 'We must take part in this gender balance movement, because if our men do not respect our women and our women cannot say no to sex, then it is not just the women who are dying but ourselves and our sons and daughters as well.'

Second, it has become clear that individualistic messages about changed sexual behaviour are ineffective. Mass public education campaigns and top-down preaching have been shown to increase levels of information, but to have little impact on people's behaviour. Rather, it is participatory, locally generated methods of identifying problems and their solutions that have been shown to result in change at the level of community.[5]

Third, a society's vulnerability to HIV/Aids is closely bound up with its lack of ability to resist global economic forces, including the results of structural adjustment, the debt burden, privatization of services, and World Trade Organization (WTO) policies on intellectual property rights, trade and services. Corruption at national level can be seen as the result of loss of autonomy of national governments, and the feeling (described by Zambians and others) that you are caught up in a spiral of increasing poverty from which there is no escape.

care and prevention

The Churches were among the first to respond to the HIV epidemic. Some Roman Catholic and Salvation Army care programmes, in particular, are numbered among the flagship Aids-care programmes in the world, and in many places, church hospitals and clinics treated people with Aids at a time when government facilities were turning them away. However, while accepting the need to build local capacity to run home-based care programmes, development agencies have generally resisted getting involved with clinics and hospitals. The really vital thing, they hold, is to prevent the spread of HIV, particularly to the next generation. The priority then becomes education and prevention, with a strong focus on young people.

In recent years it has become clear that this is not an either/or choice. It has become an internationally accepted criterion of good practice that care and prevention must go together. The best possible context for a prevention programme is one where people who have Aids are accepted and looked after. The most effective prevention strategies are those that take place in the context of an open acceptance of people with HIV/Aids, and the active participation in educational programmes of people who are themselves living with HIV. This means that a culture needs to be created in which people can be open about their status. Harriet or Joel are much more likely to 'come out' as HIV positive people if they are going to receive help, acceptance and care. If they expect to be stigmatized, marginalized or even murdered, then why should they put themselves through the agony of disclosure?

But people living with HIV are not just 'the other', the opportunity for 'the rest of us' to exercise compassion, understanding and care. They are a key element in prevention activities, because they can speak from experience. The late David Randall, the Anglican priest who started CARA Counselling, used to talk about being invited to address the pupils at his old school, and the electric effect it had. No amount of preaching and information, he said, could have equalled the impact on today's boys of his own personal story as somebody living with HIV, and his commitment to the struggle against HIV/Aids. That is why GIPA (the greater involvement of people with HIV/Aids) has become an internationally accepted principle of good practice. Good practice involves:

- care
- prevention
- counselling
- open involvement by people living with HIV/Aids.

a problem of definition

Public and local responses to HIV/Aids have been shown to be most effective where there is open and trusting collaboration between government, Churches and the rest of civil society. But this is not always easy to achieve. 'All the secular agencies are interested in are mass advertising and condoms,' said a Tanzanian bishop, 'so how can we be expected to work alongside them?' 'The Churches,' said a friend from the World Health Organization's (WHO) Aids programme, 'are completely impossible to work with because their agenda and their language have nothing to do with the real problem.'

The early Aids programmes tended to be run as semi-autonomous NGOs. Today, there is a growing realization that local worshipping communities are the places where the real challenges of care and prevention are experienced, and it is here that capacity needs building. But churches face structural challenges in addressing issues of HIV. Liturgies, homiletics and biblical studies may be felt to have very little to do with the reality of people's relationships.[6] If church communities see themselves as 'ghettos for the good', then they will not be an inclusive and welcoming environment for somebody with a fatal STI. Mainstream churches are generally male-led, and yet it is crucial for the struggle against HIV/Aids that women should be involved in leadership and programme planning. Churches which run with this challenge, as many are doing, have often found themselves engaged in painful journeys of self-discovery.[7]

There are further problems when it comes to negotiating the interface between people's everyday lives and their faith communities, and between Churches and secular organizations. The Church is not a development agency. Its primary commitment is to the living God, and to the Christ who comes among us as one who serves. Its mission is to translate the good news of that God's kingdom into human history.

What do the last two sentences have to do with what has gone before? As a Christian working in this field, I often get the feeling that I am operating within two structures of meaning, or paradigms, each with its own concepts, language and tests for truth. These can be defined, clumsily, as the scientific-western-secular paradigm (promoted by hospitals and international agencies) and the religious-missionary-church paradigm (promoted by churches, mosques and temples). In the interests of brevity, let us call them the secular paradigm and the mission paradigm.

'HIV is a virus,' says the secular paradigm, 'which eventually causes well-defined symptoms, and without good nutrition, adequate health care and targeted treatment will eventually result in death.' 'HIV is the result of immorality,' the mission paradigm may say, 'and Aids is your punishment.' Which, then, is the problem: a virus, or sin? What is the goal? Is it prevention of disease, or is it salvation? On the one hand are concepts such as empowerment, economic development, capacity building, structural change; on the other, one is talking about sin, salvation, prayer, acceptance and unconditional love.

Understanding the above dichotomy is helpful, but it is not the whole solution. HIV involves an area of human experience that is both highly intimate, deeply embedded in cultural assumptions, and at home with neither the secular nor the mission paradigm. The experience of HIV/Aids brings us to the very heart of the dilemmas over language, definition and meaning. The voices coming from that context may not be much talked about, and they may be very different from the scientific ones around which 'official' understandings are constructed. They are also different from the religious ones that characterize the Churches' definitions. These 'other' voices are the voices of culture, which may impose a different set of meanings and of definitions altogether. 'When I am at the hospital,' I was told by a trainee priest in Kenya, 'I think HIV is a virus. When I am at church, I think it is because of sin. But when I go back to my village, I think it is the curse of the ancestors for selling out our culture to the West.'

The late Dr Jonathan Mann, formerly Director of WHO's Global Aids Programme, used to quote anthropologist Mary Douglas: 'The definition of the problem determines the way we solve the problem.' In analysing the success or otherwise of HIV strategies, we need to take note of paradigm differences of understanding about the meaning of AIDS (or development, or anything else for that matter). If your answer has nothing to do with my question, then it is no help to me whatever and I shall probably ignore it.

looking forward

And so the world moves into the twenty-first century. HIV/Aids will not go away, any more than cholera or meningitis have done, but it will not be an epidemic forever: no epidemic is. Eventually, the sense of emergency fades, society itself changes a bit, the residue of the problem is mainstreamed into 'business as usual', and the attention of the world moves on to something else. From a church perspective, what then are the main development challenges emerging from the experience of HIV?

I have mentioned the global ones: the issue of debt; the related tragedy unfolding in the privatized health, education and welfare systems of the South; the growing economic marginalization of poor people in the developing world, and the ways in which this is being fanned by the policies of the WTO and the international financial institutions. More contextually, there is the socio-economic empowerment of women, and the massive burden of care and support for those who are sick and those who survive them.

And then there is death. In some countries, half a generation is being swept away and health and education systems disabled by the numbers of the sick and by the early death of young, skilled professionals. Families are made destitute, and there are millions and millions of orphaned children. By 2005, orphaned children will constitute 10 per cent of the Zambian population.[8]

In terms of development, there are two key questions. The first is: how can we create societies where people are motivated to avoid HIV, and develop participatory methodologies to help them work out how to do it? The second is: what is going to be left behind when all these young professionals, these young skilled people, these young parents, have died?

The issue of orphans is a particularly complex and difficult one, with long-term security and development implications. It falls between government departments, and may therefore be invisible in terms of official priorities. It is not accessible to easy solutions. And every parent I have ever spoken with, if they are knowingly living with Aids, has echoed Harriet's words: 'What I really worry about is, what will happen to my children and my grandchildren?'

There are orphans and street children, in growing numbers, on the streets of every major city in the world. These young people are a massive challenge to local communities, where every programme run by every agency, government or otherwise, needs to be monitored for its effect on the orphan population. Solutions need thought, planning, consultation, networking with other organizations, new resources, and the development of appropriate models of action. But if nobody steps in to help build the capacity of local communities and extended families for coping with the survivors of those who have died of HIV/Aids, then the effects of this most distressing of epidemics will be felt, in wasted talents and social disintegration, for generations to come.

conclusion: recommendations for Government

The following points are offered as areas around which further action is needed. Although the recommendations are directed at Government, they are also relevant to those agencies providing long-term care and provision to those with HIV/Aids.

- Treat HIV/Aids as an emergency, and its social consequences as long-term development issues.
- Mainstream HIV/Aids in development policy, monitoring new and existing work in relation to HIV concerns, particularly the existence of orphans. Integrate questions about HIV/Aids into existing systems for programme planning, and for programme appraisal and monitoring.
- Review sectoral development policy for health services in relation to the concerns of people with HIV/Aids, and to national policy on mother to child transmission (MTCT).
- Where there is substantial Church or faith-group input into health service provision, review Department for International Development sectoral development policies to ensure that this is taken account of in deciding how support should be structured.
- In view of evidence that successful HIV/Aids prevention depends on a strong and collaborative relationship between governments and the organizations of civil society, ensure that support for Churches and other NGOs forms part of its HIV/Aids strategy.
- Note the impact of debt, structural adjustment and international trading negotiations on the poorest people, and their implications for HIV transmission rates.
- Promote trading agreements that ensure greater availability of essential drugs and medical equipment for developing countries.

chapter 6

the environment

treading more lightly on the earth

David Gosling

introduction

Insofar as the phenomenon of globalization necessarily involves international relationships, any discussion of world development must be set within the context of the structures that determine these. Such structures are largely economic, and may be beneficial or harmful to the poor and vulnerable in any society. But they are known, and have been the subject of discussions by governments, Churches and many other bodies for several years. We shall consider the environment first within this international economic context (in which it is most likely to be taken seriously) and then independently of it in order to see what further aspects need to be addressed. We shall also examine the notion of human development so as to enlarge its scope to cover a wider range of deprivations (including environmental ones) than are usually associated with poverty.

The last major Synod report on world development (in 1986) reviewed the most significant international economic gains and losses and concluded that although many of the dire predictions of the 1960s and 1970s had not materialized, much remained to be done. India and China were cited as 'the giants which, for all the ambiguities and ambivalences, remind us of the possibilities that lie within even the most disastrous situation . . . countries where it is possible to see progress that 10 years ago would have seemed literally impossible'.[1] Rejecting the simplistic view of a Christian response based on charity and aid, the report identified the main causes of world impoverishment in terms of unjust international structures that must be challenged and changed.[2]

The international structures most closely associated with world poverty are trading relationships, the international monetary system and the mechanisms whereby the rich countries use their power (and ultimately their military power) against the poor and the weak. To give an example of the manner in which an unjust trading relationship can increase poverty, we may cite the Common Agricultural Policy (CAP) of the European Union, whereby the EU trades with the developing and other parts of the world. This discourages imports of fruit and vegetables from developing countries while at the same time enabling European nations to dump their own surpluses at low prices wherever they choose (which may also be where they are least needed). The results are obvious: income and jobs are lost in the developing countries, essential foods cost more in Europe, and the dumping of European surpluses further restricts exports from the developing world. If globalization meant an end to such injustices, then we might welcome it, but this seems highly unlikely. But now we must add another dimension to this entire area: what are the *environmental* implications of trade relationships?

An environmental critique of international trade will ask questions that economists have traditionally ignored. For example, how essential is the total 'quantity' of certain types of trade? Bearing in mind their capacity for pollution, their dependence on non-renewable fuels and the risk they pose to human life – especially to children in urban areas – do we need so much international trade in motor vehicles? Of course the car industry worldwide employs large numbers of skilled people whose livelihoods should not be jeopardized without good reason, but our question remains a legitimate one. And what of the international tobacco trade, now that we have conclusive scientific evidence that tobacco smoking is damaging to the health not only of those who indulge in it, but to others as well? We must also decide whether we will continue to take the results of scientific research seriously, or proceed according to a preconceived ideological agenda which disparages science – as has become increasingly characteristic of the environmental lobby.

Jubilee 2000 and the environment

The Jubilee 2000 campaign, in which the Churches played a significant part, was largely successful in persuading governments to cancel or reschedule the debts of developing countries to the international banks. It is to be hoped that this momentum will be maintained because much still remains to be done, and because church members who take part in such campaigns learn a great deal from them about the role of justice in international affairs. There is also an important environmental dimension to this issue.

In the mid-1980s, a sub-unit of the World Council of Churches (WCC) conducted the first studies of the ethical and theological implications of international debt. The arguments laid great emphasis on the environmental consequences of international economic relationships between the mid-1940s, when the so-called Bretton Woods instruments (the World Bank, the IMF and the GATT tariffs body) were set up, and the mid-1980s. They concluded that debt cancellation was not a matter of 'forgiveness', as some Western aid organizations had maintained, but of justice, because, had there been a 'polluter pays' principle from the outset, the cost to the industrial nations of the North would at least have equalled the total amount of money borrowed by the developing world.[3] The WCC as a whole did not endorse these arguments, but they resurfaced in the presentation of the Council of Churches for Britain and Ireland (now Churches Together in Britain and Ireland) at the Earth Summit in 1992.[4]

In a country such as Brazil the repayment of debts to the international banks takes place primarily via the export of cash crops which are desired but not necessarily needed by the rich nations. Repayment of loans must occur in a hard currency and with interest, which means that it can only take place via foreign exchange earned through exports. In passing, it might be worth noting that if globalization meant that such debts could be repaid in 'any' currency, then it might be welcomed. But, as we remarked earlier, this is very unlikely to happen.

Cash crops grow best on large plantations, many of which are created by cutting down forests, which also produces timber for export. Cash crop cultivation may be enhanced by the use of new strains of seeds, fertilizers and pesticides, all of which can cause long-term environmental problems such as toxic residues and illness among plantation workers. Furthermore, the loss of forest cover reduces biodiversity and the capacity of trees to absorb carbon dioxide.

Cancellation of the debts of developing countries such as Brazil to the international banks can therefore cause major environmental improvements. And it should be pointed out that this is done not as a matter of 'forgiveness' or charity, but of justice.

The World Bank is some distance removed from such thinking, though its understanding of poverty and development has recently undergone a significant shift. The most recent World Development Report defines poverty not just in economic terms, but as a multidimensional problem that includes powerlessness, vulnerability and fear in addition to lack of food, shelter and other economic necessities.[5] The removal of poverty, therefore, requires not just economic growth but also security and empowerment, which implies strengthening the ability of the poor to remove inhibiting factors such as discrimination and inequity (e.g. between men and women). This is a welcome move in the direction of justice.

Both trading relationships and the international banking system illustrate the means whereby rich countries wield their power in relation to the poor. But there are additional mechanisms, as when, for example, the British Aid and Trade Provision (ATP) has been used to subsidize uncompetitive exports. Thus the Indian government was once told that unless it bought British helicopters it did not want, useful British aid would be jeopardized.[6] More extreme examples of the use of political power by the rich nations are the NATO wars against Iraq and the Serbs. Whatever the rights and wrongs of these confrontations, the environmental cost has been enormous.

We have briefly considered international trade, the banks and other relationships between rich and poor nations – the international developmental agenda – from the perspective of their environmental implications. We now consider particular environmental issues in more detail.

climate change

The 1992 Earth Summit and the 1997 Kyoto Protocol set out international targets for reducing greenhouse gas emissions, which are now known to cause enhanced global warming. These targets require the industrial nations to reduce their emissions by about 5 per cent by the year 2012.

The connections between global warming and climate change are highly complex, and scientists believe that the consequences of the former may vary considerably from place to place. In Britain, for example, it is possible that weather patterns may alter dramatically if changes occur in the delicately balanced Gulf Stream mechanism which influences weather fronts as they impinge upon the western side of our islands.

Important issues on the international climate change agenda are whether or not rich countries which emit more than their share of greenhouse gases (e.g. the USA) can buy an entitlement to do so from countries which emit less (carbon emissions trading), and whether or not the planting of more trees really makes much difference to the total quantity of atmospheric carbon dioxide. Literature about these issues is readily available elsewhere.[7]

There are, however, three vital questions which scientists from a range of scientific disciplines, politicians and others must consider very carefully. First, what rate of climate change poses serious risks to human health and to the environment, and how do we determine it? Second, can we control the climate in order to avoid such dangers? Third, if we cannot control the climate so as to avoid serious risks to human health and the environment, can we shape the future to accommodate the anticipated climate change?

These questions are extremely important, and they place the environment firmly on the national and international developmental agenda. The failure of the post-Kyoto climate change meetings at The Hague in November 2000 is a major setback. The basic problem is that people in the rich industrial nations, especially the USA and Canada, collectively refuse to make any changes in their standards of living to offset the prospect of major disruptions in the global climate. Even though they themselves will suffer (for example, Florida is racked by increasingly severe hurricanes), they bury their heads in the sand and ridicule the bearers of bad news, that is, the scientists. If one good thing did come out of the global conference at The Hague, it is that nobody now doubts the existence of global warming. But some of the participants did not believe in the links between it and climate change, and some in both categories simply refused to envisage any realistic action to improve matters.

expanding human capabilities

Economic poverty is only one of a number of fundamental deprivations that must be removed in order to promote true human development, which is an imperative for the Christian. This has been emphasized recently by Amartya Sen, who defines development as 'the expansion of real freedoms that the citizens enjoy to pursue the objectives that they have reason to value . . . the expansion of human capability'.[8]

This view of human development is not new, and political economists such as John Stuart Mill would have had no difficulty with it. But during the years between the Second World War and the present day the concept of development has been dominated by overemphasis on growth in real income. It has also been naively assumed that growth in real income per head is proportional to the national income divided by the total population. We know that national wealth does not 'trickle down' equitably to the poor.

Among the various fundamental human deprivations we must include the environmental ones that are experienced particularly acutely by the poorer communities of the developing world. The level of pollution of air, water and land in the city of Cubatão in Brazil, for example, has to be experienced to be believed. The only dissenting voices raised against such appalling industrial side-effects are those of Roman Catholic clergy who read out during Sunday Mass the death certificates of all those whose deaths can be attributed to pollution.[9]

If we understand development to include the removal of all fundamental deprivations, then we can bring together the full range of economic and environmental constraints that stultify human capabilities. In a recent interview, Amartya Sen enlarged on this view as follows:

> Poverty is deprivation of human freedom: among the factors that can make us substantively less free there are a number of different considerations including lowness of income, lack of basic education, lack of arrangement for health care, on one side; but also on the other an adverse environment, a depleted natural resource base, foul air to breathe, or polluted rivers to get your water from. So ecology comes into the notion of human poverty in a big way. It's not a notion of 'ecological' poverty as such; it is part of the general notion of poverty. People might sometimes complain that I try to integrate the idea of ecology with the idea of development. If that is the charge, I plead guilty. I do intend to do it, and for exactly the same reasons for which Gro Harlem Brundtland in the Brundtland Report made the basic concept of the environment integral to the notion of sustainable development. Sustainability on the one side is referring to its environmental viability (among other things), and development on the other hand is the motivating end product, which is the motivating factor in making us take an interest in the environment. I see no conflict whatsoever in taking such a broad view of development and ecology, and at the same time believing, as I do, that I take ecology extremely seriously.[10]

Consistent with his view of development as the expansion of human capabilities is Sen's argument for a broad and participative interpretation of economic development which takes into account the need to expand social opportunities. He recognizes that where social opportunities already exist, the enlargement of markets can significantly enhance them, but that most people are excluded from benefits through lack of literacy and education, together with other capabilities associated with basic health, social security, gender equality, land rights and local democracy. Such a total view of human development is much more consistent with a Christian understanding of it than the narrow economic one. 'Man shall not live by bread alone . . .'

a Christian approach

A Christian approach to the deterioration of the physical condition of our planet must operate at many levels. The problems must be analysed internationally, nationally and locally, our responses must take place at all these levels, and both our analysis and our responses must be informed by the resources agreed as authoritative by most mainstream Churches – scripture, tradition, and our best modern knowledge (e.g. science). We can do no more here than outline some of these.

We have indicated that the removal of the unjust structures known to be responsible for world impoverishment – especially though not exclusively in developing countries – can have important positive environmental consequences. Less international trade based on scarce and non-renewable natural resources that may cause local pollution in the process of being extracted (e.g. minerals, coal, oil, etc.), less trade in non-essential goods that may be polluting or harmful to health (e.g. tobacco products), and less advertising designed to stimulate such trade, will be environmentally beneficial. The campaign to remove international debt must be continued both for the reasons originally given, but also for environmental reasons. Bodies such as the World Bank and the IMF should be encouraged to take seriously the welfare economics of Amartya Sen and others who try to extend the notion of impoverishment to include the full range of human deprivations, including ecological ones. The World Bank has already made a start in this direction.

The mechanisms that prevent rich nations from oppressing poorer ones need to be strengthened through support for bodies such as the UN. The environmental consequences of all wars are disastrous, quite apart from the tragic loss of life. Christians must enter into all these vital international areas to press for justice along the full range of environment, development and peace issues. They cannot be content, therefore, with the narrower agenda of the environmental organizations. However, it must be acknowledged that these have done important work in challenging the excesses of the multinationals. Globalization must be judged by whether or not it promotes international justice. The initial indications are ominous – a view set out recently in more detail by a group of Roman Catholic scholars.[11]

National agendas will be governed to a large extent by what is happening internationally. Thus, for example, while a national government might temporarily cushion a petroleum price hike by the oil producers, it cannot justify long-term subsidies of the real prices of non-renewable fuels. Why should the Churches not use their considerable educational resources to ensure that people understand the non-renewable and polluting properties of the full range of energy sources? And while we are on this subject, might it not be a good idea to encourage reduced greenhouse gas production at the same time as lowering the speeds of vehicles in built-up areas to save lives (especially of children)? That's adding an environmental to a develop-mental issue at the local level.

A major obstacle to environmentally responsible living is the power of advertising to promote consumerism. The ideology of limitless consumption has become the dominant creed of many large corporations, as the following claim by a sales analyst in the USA makes clear:

> Our enormously productive economy . . . demands that we make consumption our way of life, that we convert the buying and use of goods into rituals, that we seek spiritual satisfaction, our ego satisfaction, in consumption. We need things consumed, burned up, worn out, replaced and discarded on an ever-increasing rate.[12]

Churches must resist such propaganda by educating their members about the greed, acquisitiveness and individualism that underlie such assertions. Unfortunately some churches virtually baptize the current mood of secular individualism by ignoring the social dimension of Christianity.

Much can be done by churches to set an example in the way they use their property and generally conduct their affairs. It is now possible for any church building to have an energy audit and for advice to be given as to the best way to conserve energy and reduce heating costs. Church schools can similarly be encouraged to conserve energy and use renewable energy sources (some do already). Clergy can be encouraged to use public transport and/or bicycles instead of cars. New forms of burial using woodland areas instead of churchyards can be experimented with. There is enormous scope for new forms of liturgy with an environmental focus (e.g. imaginative Eucharists, harvest festivals), for new hymns and ecologically friendly congregations ('eco-congregations').[13]

Many people, churchgoers among them, undertake a variety of activities that are environmentally beneficial and should be encouraged. These include the separation of domestic waste into biodegradable and non-biodegradable components, paper recycling, the recycling of goods (e.g. clothes) at charity shops (e.g. Oxfam), the selective purchase of foodstuffs (e.g. avoidance of Nescafé products), lower meat consumption, increased use of public transport and bicycles, energy saving, improved energy efficiency (e.g. insulation) and a host of similar sensible measures. There are no sound scientific reasons to suppose that organically produced foods are preferable to non-organically produced ones, or that the genetically modified products that reach the shops pose any risks for human consumption (e.g. cherry tomatoes). Unfortunately the same cannot be said for the beef that was so enthusiastically promoted during the 1980s or for foods that contain monosodium glutamate.

All the major world religions presuppose closeness between God, humanity and nature (or humanity and nature in the case of Theravada Buddhism). The Judaeo-Christian tradition expresses the creative character of God in terms of an ongoing sustaining relationship with the creation that is paralleled by a lesser one between humanity and the natural world. The natural world can therefore never be equal to human life (as in the Gaia hypothesis), but it possesses intrinsic value and the potential for ultimate liberation – the transfiguration of creation, as the Orthodox liturgy so evocatively expresses it.

Anglicanism adopts a sacramental understanding of the natural world whereby matter, in relation to God, possesses both the symbolic function of expressing God's mind, and the instrumental function whereby humankind pursues God's ongoing creative activity. William Temple, Charles Raven, and before them George Herbert and Thomas Traherne, are the main proponents of this view, which deserves much more attention than it has received in recent years.

Christians have a heritage that should put them into the forefront of concern to preserve and nourish our world, and they must mobilize the resources of Scripture, tradition, the best human knowledge and our collective human energies to do so.

chapter 7

the role of business in development

Peter Malcolm

global development – an introduction

International (Jeremy Bentham's prescient word) development means securing improved health, education and training, infrastructure, partnerships, capacity building, opportunity, business development, and much else. All are essential to enable people in poorer countries to develop materially and spiritually, play a fuller part in the world and have better lives. Health issues, malnutrition, the HIV/Aids epidemic, malaria, TB, and other diseases in the developing world, must continue to be addressed with vigour by the international community, including business. Most obviously we should retain a sharp focus upon the basic, yet key, requirement of ensuring a pure water supply for everyone. The effects of the all-too-prevalent wars and drought in parts of the developing world have compounded the problems and led to famine despite laudable alleviation efforts. The issues of global population size (1900: 1.2 billion; 1960: 3 billion; 2000: 6 billion; 2030: estimated 9 billion) and birth control remain pressing and challenging.

This chapter draws on the submission by the Confederation of British Industry (CBI) to the White Paper on Globalisation and Development of December 2000 and covers globalization, investment, trade, business views on multilateral initiatives, export credits, aid and debt and corporate social responsibility. Business wants developing countries to share the many benefits of globalization through an extension of that process and their fuller integration into the global economy. A truly multi-functional approach such as the one urged by the CBI offers the best chance of securing those objectives. Business remains fully engaged and committed to doing all in its power towards that end.

The CBI values its close liaison with the Department for International Development (DfID). In 1997 it gave supportive business views on DfID's initial development White Paper and welcomed recognition of its key role. The first for 20 years, this White Paper set out policies to reduce global poverty significantly by 2015, achieve sustainable development and create partnerships with developing countries on the basis of specific and achievable targets. Business collaboration also remained a key element within the December 2000 White Paper.

globalization

The CBI is convinced that developmental objectives, including long-term improvement in living standards and health, can only be secured through the wealth created by more global trade and investment. Globalization is the proven wealth-creating process of the liberalized, post-exchange control, closely knit world economy, in which change is a key feature. It has led *inter alia* to mobility of capital, labour, entrepreneurial activity, trade, investment, technology, better working practices, services, tourism and even, very basically, benefits such as all-year-round fresh produce. Greater understanding of other peoples through improved communications has also resulted, certainly among those using the world's business, scientific, international media and perhaps dominant cultural language, English. Karl Sauvant of UNCTAD (the United Nations Conference on Trade and Development) has said that foreign direct investment, even more than trade, is leading to an integrated international production system and the internationalization of domestic policy agenda – with developmental benefit. The greatest tragedy remains that the advantages of globalization and international capitalism enjoyed by the developed world are not reaching enough of the world's poor. Our main challenge is, therefore, to integrate them more effectively into that process so that they are no longer deprived of its benefits. Yet by attacking globalization this is what some seem to argue for.

The UK's abandonment of its exchange control regime in 1979 was only one important milestone, and certainly hardly the actual genesis of the current process of accelerating globalization. In the 1960s the CBI had commissioned research by Professor Brian Reddaway, Director of Applied Economics at Cambridge, which demonstrated that British investment overseas did not take place at the expense of investment in the UK. Opportunities anywhere determined investment location.[1] In reality, allowing resources to go towards growing markets and opportunities is the only way to preserve wealth and satisfy material needs. Investment flows beneficially allow capital, good management and labour practices, ideas, technology, research and more to move around the world.

The UK's imperial history and its support for 'free' trade from the nineteenth century onwards spread its culture – helped by, among other things, its missionaries. British people and businesses became accustomed to extensive involvement in trade and investment around the globe – in both the 'pink parts' and elsewhere. Indigenous cultures and traditions were not, in the main, deliberately targeted for attack in that process. Before 1914, nearly half of Britain's wealth was invested overseas; now, the increasingly large number of inward investors in the UK are given a warm welcome and encouraged to participate fully in our economy and institutions. As the second highest foreign investor after the USA (although in 1999 the UK's foreign direct investment (FDI) of $199 billion was actually higher than the USA's $151 billion), it would ill behove the UK to do otherwise. In that respect, we do precisely the same as all developing countries seeking capital and the other advantages of globalization. Even the CBI (like the UK itself) has changed as a result of the process. It is no longer an organization of manufacturers only but now represents in its membership all sectors of the economy (roughly one-half its members are in manufacturing, the other half in commerce) and – importantly – companies in the UK totally irrespective of their nationality. Many developing countries also increasingly benefit, to varying degrees, from globalization, through their own multinational investors and traders.

Companies operate in a fast-changing world. The CBI believes the tremendous changes in information technology and electronic communications offer poorer countries a great opportunity and the potential to increase their integration into the global economy. Specifically, the staggering expansion, actual and projected, of mobile and other telephony (despite Africa's present shortage), development of the Internet, growth of electronic business, global key skill development, outsourcing and the use of call centres, will all facilitate integration in ways governments are incapable of addressing.

international investment

The CBI recognized early that international trade and investment were two sides of the same coin and that the liberalization of both remains the only way to generate the wealth needed for global development. The greatly enhanced private FDI flows currently seen throughout the global economy – at well over $300 billion, such flows are many times higher than government overseas development assistance – have significantly enhanced the role of business in international development. Practically all countries wish for and seek to attract such flows and their benefits and therefore compete for FDI. Between 1990 and 1998, FDI flows to developing countries more than doubled, to $50 billion. However, over half went to only a few of them:

Singapore, for example, received more than the whole of Africa put together. How can we ensure that others also receive more investment? First, developing countries must show that they are welcoming, encouraging of, and taking positive steps to promote, entrepreneurial activity, including liberalization and privatization. Second, they must also maximize their key 'selling points' – skills, unique traditions, communications, infrastructure and residential and tourist attractiveness. As one positive way forward, Clare Short, the UK Development Secretary, has suggested that pension funds should invest more in private equity in developing countries in a 'socially responsible way'. She has pointed out that investment of pension funds in East Asia over the past 30 years has contributed to 'the fastest reduction in poverty for more people than ever before in history, cutting the proportion of people living on less than $1 a day there to under 10 per cent from 40 per cent'.[2]

FDI complements indigenous investment but cannot replace it. FDI ranges from around 5 per cent to perhaps 10 per cent of gross fixed capital formation in various parts of the world. Some countries, whilst recognizing and supporting the benefits of free capital flow, believe that in the shorter term the flight of indigenous savings to 'safer havens' elsewhere remains a problem. As a result, not all have yet freed their capital controls. More, however, enthusiastically and fully participate in the 'liberalization' process in all its facets. This is perhaps in part a result of an implicit recognition of their having mistakenly and tragically embraced now discredited political ideology during the early years of the post-colonial period, often at the expense of economic progress, free markets, democratic institutions and potentially beneficial engagement in the global economy.

international trade

The CBI judges the World Trade Organization (WTO) (and earlier the GATT) to have been remarkably successful for over 50 years. Nearly all countries recognize the advantages of membership. The WTO is a rules-based membership organization, offering special and differential treatment for developing country members (the majority), capacity building, legal advice, technical assistance and funding provided by developed countries. Other benefits include further liberalization in markets for goods and services, and examination of the 'new' issues such as environmental and labour standards. In 1998, world merchandise exports were worth over $5 trillion – nearly 20 times higher than in 1948 when the GATT was founded. Business was, therefore, disappointed at the failure of the WTO Ministerial in Seattle in 1999, caused, not by misguided protesters and demonstrators, but through inadequate preparation, procedural deficiencies and certain unfortunately timed public pronouncements.

Developing countries need a comprehensive trade round – what Clare Short has called a 'Development Round' – to be complementary to, and compatible with, their ongoing efforts to collaborate regionally on the basis of economically viable areas. However, more than just a new WTO agreement will be needed to ensure that the poorest people benefit from the increased wealth arising through international trade and investment facilitation. Complex social, cultural, historical and other factors continue to stand in the way of such development. Although the WTO includes some of the world's poorest countries, for example Mozambique, Bangladesh and Mauritania, it must be extended quickly to all eligible countries. China is likely to join shortly, and, in time, Russia. Some argue that there are no beneficial effects of 'trickle-down' of development aid and investment funding in developing countries – a perception rejected by the CBI. UK trade policy, subsumed into, and influential within, that of the EU, has long been felt by the British government to help developing countries. Despite their problems, it is worth noting that such countries' exports expanded by 8.5 per cent in 1999 – around twice as fast as the global average.

The CBI and European business have recognized that some developed countries' agricultural policies impede the efforts of developing and newly industrializing countries to secure more trade and that textile trade also remains particularly sensitive. In September 2000 the European Commission proposed to go beyond all previous EU commitments by granting unrestricted duty-free access to all products except arms from all least developed countries. This is essentially what many had hoped might emerge from the EU at the Seattle WTO Ministerial.

Trade facilitation is another issue on which progress had been expected at Seattle – touching on improving trade and customs procedures and the elimination of 'red tape'. Business has discussed these issues with customs officers from many developing countries who were disappointed that their progress on trade facilitation was not translated into a WTO agreement. Another important step in international development will be the accession of the current list of European Union candidate members, many of them developing countries. This could result, eventually, in the EU having over 500 million citizens, and much more trade – whatever the eventual institutional structure of the EU and the future of the single currency.

multilateral initiatives

The CBI works with some 300 multilateral organizations engaged in securing an integrated framework for global development. With other European business federations, it has argued for improvement in the EU's aid disbursement since the EU is the world's largest provider of multilateral development assistance. Business supports continued use of the EU's Generalized System of Preferences and the latest Cotonou Convention, helping around 70 African, Caribbean and Pacific developing countries, which was agreed in June 2000.

The CBI also works with the relevant Bretton Woods financial institutions – primarily the IMF and the World Bank group (together with UN agencies and regional development associations) – to offer business views on strengthening the international finance system. The roles of the Bank and the IMF have both been under review following external criticism by, *inter alia*, the Meltzer Commission to the US Congress, which suggested that IMF assistance be confined to middle-income countries encountering difficulties. Notwithstanding this, the IMF is likely to remain a lender of last resort to developing and other countries.

Business feels that any lowering or delay in payment of US contributions to the IMF as a result of Meltzer would be a serious setback. James Wolfensohn, the Bank President, and Horst Kohler, Managing Director of the IMF, have sought to improve their collaboration through a joint declaration redefining respective responsibilities on the institutional, structural and social dimensions. This confirms the Bank's poverty reduction role and programme focus, particularly where the private sector is unable to help. The IMF will concentrate on systemic issues related to the functioning of financial markets and crisis prevention, providing international financial and macroeconomic stability and, in crises, negotiating stabilization and reform programmes.

Business welcomes this cooperation, the establishment of a new financial sector liaison committee and streamlined loan conditions. It supports all international efforts to encourage developing countries' capacity building – so that poorer peoples and countries acquire an ability to cope and participate more effectively in an increasingly complex world.

Priorities remain education and training and greater recognition of rights and opportunities, including technical assistance, trade remedies and disputes settlement.

export credits, aid and debt

Trade finance provision, too, has a key developmental role. The main activity of the DTI's Export Credit Guarantee Department (ECGD) is to provide credit insurance and financial support for UK capital goods and project exports typically sold on medium and long terms of payment to developing and other countries at no cost to the UK taxpayer. This type of finance is essential for securing developmental objectives because the private sector is currently unable to absorb the risks associated with long-term capital goods projects in developing countries. The ECGD, like the World Bank's specialist agency MIGA, also provides investment insurance, again of great importance and relevance to global development.[3]

The matter of linkages between Government aid and export credit support, provided on a 'commercial' basis, remains a key question for the future. Some countries, unlike the UK, continue to use such mixed credits. The 1997 White Paper withdrew the former Aid and Trade Provision but offered the prospect of mixed credits in country programmes. DfID, however, is quite clearly unconvinced of their value and has no intention of using them. Meanwhile, efforts to untie aid have been unsuccessful in the OECD as a result of veto by the Japanese (with the largest aid budget of over £10 billion) and the French, leading to calls for UK unilateral untying. The CBI has re-emphasized the principle, hitherto accepted by all, that a prerequisite for untying should remain multilateral agreement.

Business knows that a high proportion of some developing countries' income is required to pay interest on their debts and supports attempts to address the problem of Third World debt within the heavily indebted poor countries initiative (the HIPC). We feel that countries with properly monitored structural reform programmes should be assisted – but that earlier loans, had they been used better by recipients, should have produced earning assets. Debt is not, in itself, necessarily bad. It would certainly not have helped developing countries had they been deprived of British capital goods and much-needed project cover because the ECGD (to whom developing countries are indebted), unlike its counterparts in other countries, had been unable to provide finance. This situation was, happily, largely avoided by the

Government's recent positive review of the ECGD. If countries were generally to become aware that debts could be forgiven irrespective of real need or too easily, there would be a greater inclination towards default. The CBI also feels that country debt restructuring and 'burden sharing' by private creditors in the 'London Club' is unfairly affected by IMF restructuring, whereas that does not apply to official public creditors in the 'Paris Club'.

The British government now requires the ECGD to operate under a revised mission statement and 'business principles', taking human rights, sustainable development, business integrity and good governance into account. Business supports these laudable objectives but strongly believes that the main purpose of the ECGD must remain to ensure that UK firms are given backing to compete effectively against exporters and investors supported by government-backed export credit agencies in other countries.

corporate social responsibility

International business remains involved with, and takes a progressive view towards, its corporate social responsibility (CSR), which is good for business efficiency, staff and public relations. Others, however, mistakenly see CSR as a panacea for development, whereas it really depends on wealth creation. CSR has properly been put in the spotlight through globalization and includes the appropriate business contribution to development. Pressures remain upon business to be even more accountable for its social and environmental activities and to address human rights and other sensitive political issues in the developing world. Development, relationships with contractors and supply-chain issues including overseas sourcing of goods for Western markets, the retreat of the state, and the rise of civil society, all impact upon CSR.

Business recognizes the risk to its reputation posed by negative consumer reaction and media exposure of any perceived corporate 'misdeeds' and has responded positively, by adopting the highest standards and accepting wider responsibilities. It believes it has sometimes faced misguided pressure from environmental non-government organizations (NGOs). One example of this was the Brent Spa debacle. An oil rig was towed across the sea at great expense for costly dismantling following NGO pressure against its disposal or 'dumping' at sea in case it contained polluting remnants of oil, which was denied. It transpired that, in fact, it contained so little oil that disposal at sea would have been far less environmentally damaging and expensive. The lesson is surely that such matters should be left to those who know the science, the technology and the facts.

International Codes of Conduct have also emerged, together with ongoing community 'outreach' by business. These include such measures as the International Labour Organization principles and the OECD voluntary guide-lines for medium national enterprises, together with the latter's convention on combating the bribery of foreign public officials. Governments too have taken a number of initiatives, such as closer DfID liaison with business and work by the Foreign and Commonwealth Office Global Citizenship Unit and the Cabinet Office Performance and Innovation Unit. The CBI increasingly briefs its members on CSR and the latest thinking and developments on the responsibilities of companies, both legally, and in the wider sense of embracing all stakeholders and society.

The Prime Minister has spoken publicly to the CBI of the need to address green issues and global environmental problems through a partnership between business, Government and civil society. He put business at the heart of effective solutions to environmental dilemmas, citing examples of resource efficiency and the development of clean technologies from some of the largest UK companies. He committed resources to research into wind power, low carbon technology, and providing export-clean technology using the Kyoto Convention. Business welcomes the Government's commitment and is pursuing the dialogue with the Prime Minister.

Export controls also reflect widely accepted policies and give welcome guidance to business, finance providers and others on strategic, security and other accepted reasons for restrictions on exports. This policy incorpo-rates CSR, development, 'ethical trade' and environmental and social standards. Business supports it and works with all Government depart-ments involved.

HIV/Aids

Business regards the global HIV/Aids epidemic with great concern, particularly its devastating effects upon developing countries, where over 90 per cent of the 6 million new HIV infections each year occur. In sub-Saharan African countries, population is likely to be hard hit over the next 20 years – at 698 million, 61 million lower than without Aids. Economic growth could be cut by a quarter in the worst affected sectors, including transport, mining, agriculture, fishing, tourism and construction. Earlier entry by children into the labour market, retention of older workers, large numbers of orphans, political and social instability and reduced family incomes are all feared. Business has acted responsibly through preventive education of employees, review of employment conditions and management of ill health in the workforce. CBI members in the pharmaceutical, medical, health, education and training sectors remain heavily engaged in research aimed at remedies or protection. Consequently, although there is still no vaccine, medication now exists to lengthen and improve the quality of life of people with HIV. Sadly, expensive medicines are not affordable by poorer countries and cheaper solutions are needed, while preventive measures might be further promoted, including the wider use of condoms, and maybe even the degree of protection given by circumcision. Many wider problems remain including cost, safety, cultural obstacles, complexity of research and development, legal liability, intellectual property law, its enforcement, and the fact that investment for production can probably only occur after feasibility assessment. Business recognizes the vital need to find solutions. Globalization has helped the world understand better the fight against the HIV/Aids threat.

chapter 8
corruption

good governance vs Corruption Incorporated

Karl Ziegler

introduction

As the millennium celebrations draw to an end, the challenges of good governance remain paramount in the public eye[1]. Political funding scandals in Germany, France, the Indian sub-continent and the Far East remain topical. The funding of candidates in the USA will continue to be a contentious theme for the new administration, while a similar problem, the funding of political parties, has surfaced in the UK. Ten years ago, newspapers would have been reluctant to give details of public and private sector corruption scandals without passing their proposed copy through a battery of in-house lawyers.

As the third millennium begins, such scandals dominate world attention. People of conscience speak out more than ever before about the phenomenon. Both criminality and corruption have become globalized by venal people equipped with the latest generation of money-transferring and communication skills. Some of the world's great banks are trying to fight the problem more sincerely than others. 'Corruption Incorporated', the grey, parallel economic powerhouse that bestrides so much of the world's internal and cross-border trade, has stirred many of the world's international institutions and law makers to tighten up both national and global legislation to bridle it more effectively.

Since the late 1980s, the world has become more aware of the pernicious nation-destroying nature of institutionalized corruption. The pervasive menace of what is often described as 'grand corruption' – the use of public power for private gain – is now a major issue on the international political agenda. Its ability to destroy economies, to undermine public and private morality, to ruin ecologies and to corrode intellectual integrity has become clear.

The world's two leading multinational financial institutions, the World Bank and the IMF, used to prefer 'quiet diplomacy', behind the scenes, and only on economic matters. Their country officers could expect career advancement by putting the best possible face on their assigned nations' economic stories. According to the current President of the World Bank, James Wolfensohn, corruption is a 'cancer', one which diverts resources from the poor to the rich. It increases the cost of running businesses, distorts public expenditure and deters foreign investors. At last, the World Bank and the IMF have given clear instructions that corruption in whatever form ought not to be tolerated. Governments that steal from their people will find themselves increasingly alienated from these institutions. The world's poor will ultimately be the net beneficiaries of this new policy.

the global nature of corruption

Although now cited by many development experts as being the single greatest brake to economic growth in the world's poorest economies, corruption is hardly unfamiliar to some of the world's most prosperous economies, or to their business leaders and politicians. During the 1990s the leaders of premier financial and trading houses in Japan, Indonesia and Korea were indicted amidst a cloud of significant corruption scandals. These Asian powerhouse economies have now joined Italy, France, Spain and Germany in exposing major domestic networks of corruption. Ironically, most of these and many other leading trading nations in the West explicitly fuel corruption by permitting their exporting companies to write off, for tax purposes, the costs of bribes in winning overseas contracts. The USA is unique among Western powers with its strong legal stance towards corporate bribery. In the United States, the Foreign Corrupt Practices Act (FCPA) makes it illegal for companies to pay bribes offshore to win business. Informed businessmen say that even these rigid regulations are often circumvented via joint ventures and other mechanisms in America's offshore trading activities.

In sub-Saharan Africa generally, leadership continues to impose itself through questionable elections or military intervention. Ruling elites too often make all major economic decisions behind a cloud of unaccountability. The electorate in far too many states is effectively disenfranchised from the democratic process. Money stolen from the national purse, from Nigeria to Kenya and the Sudan to Zimbabwe, often never finds its way back home from an ever growing list of offshore 'financial centres', whose newest members often claim to offer greater anonymity for depositors than the older havens for stolen loot. Some estimates suggest that unaccountable leaders have taken 40 per cent of Africa's private wealth offshore. Many of Africa's most educated people work offshore. Both this capital flight and these skilled people are desperately needed in Africa to help facilitate genuine nation building.

The arms trade, often financed by the secret sale of 'conflict diamonds' and other untaxed resources removed from the African continent, provides rich pickings for corrupt kickbacks. The nature of the arms trade is such that 'strategic secrecy' is held by a small circle around the office of the head of state. This makes it very difficult to trace the level of bribes paid. Indeed, it represents the single greatest incentive to the perpetuity of internal repression and external conflicts.

Following the lead of the IMF in 1997, the World Bank publicly renounced the endemic corruption that had built up to an arrogant crescendo in Kenya, previously called 'Africa's Switzerland'. Both banks lost patience with the hypocrisy of Moi's government, alternately promising reforms and then repeatedly breaking its word. Since the highly suspect 're-election' of Moi in late 1992, the country has slipped into political and economic chaos. A local Kenyan cleric commented recently: 'The worst deficiency we have is that we introduced democracy without democrats.' At the end of 2000, both institutions demanded far greater transparency on the part of the Moi government. As a result an anti-corruption commission has been established, although it is feared that only junior miscreants will be exposed.

Kleptocrats from Kenya's Moi to the former Nigerian generals continue to snub their noses at reprimands from the World Bank and the IMF. Even the anti-corruption-focused President Obasanjo finds it difficult to avoid politically inspired compromises with tribally based leading figures. However, as we have seen, these international banks of last resort are drawing a line in the sand between good and bad governance, in Africa and elsewhere. They now recognize that politics and economics are interdependent throughout the world's struggling economies.

Even Uganda, whose President Museveni was seen to be providing trans-parent and accountable leadership from 1986, has been widely criticized since his country's debt relief package was put into place. Museveni's government achieved the 1997 'deal of the year' by winning the IMF and World Bank's first ever debt forgiveness package for a troubled nation-state borrower. What set Uganda's initiative apart from those demanded by many other heavily indebted nations in Africa and by Jubilee 2000 campaigners was the government's promise of ongoing accountability and frequent audit-ing over future years. Museveni's administration pledged that specific social sector targets would benefit from the proceeds of debt forgiveness. He gave an undertaking that full and frequent on-site reviews of the use of proceeds would be encouraged and honoured. Sadly, much of Uganda's early debt relief was used in the purchase of a new presidential jet and military involvement deep in the Congo.

In 1982 Mexico's debt crisis triggered an international banking crisis, the effects of which continue to be felt today. For the next ten years Mexico became a haven for speculative investment capital. Some of this investment was the laundered re-investment of funds by perhaps 50 of Mexico's leading family groups, some of it untaxed and made anonymous by offshore banks and trust companies. Mexico's list of billionaires grew from two in 1988 to 24 in 1994. The nation's leading billionaire, Carlos Slim, has more money than 17 million of his countrymen put together.

What happened in Mexico during 1982–93 was that the rich were doing very well, while investments in health, education, basic infrastructure and productive investments, to create jobs and export earnings, sagged badly. The nation's foreign debt swelled from $82 billion in 1982 to $120 billion in 1993. Rich Mexicans were exporting cash and shopping abroad, from Miami to Geneva. In 1994 a new government bit the bullet and devalued the currency by 15 per cent. Seeing this, and hooded Zapatistas with guns in the south, local and foreign speculative investors cashed in their pesos and stampeded for the exits. Like a pricked balloon, the Mexican peso lost 70 per cent of its value and foreign reserves disappeared. Mexico's economic development was put back by some ten years. The international lifeboat launched by the IMF, the World Bank, the US Treasury and others started setting conditions on the new government.

In 1997 Mexico's Institutional Revolutionary Party (PRI), the nation's dominant party for many decades, suffered a serious setback when it lost the mayorship of Mexico City. Many observers feel that continued public sector corruption, fuelled significantly by the world's largest illegal business – drug trafficking – helped to undermine the ruling party's monopoly of power. Mexico's new president, a businessman who managed to overcome the long rule of the PRI, came in on a largely anti-corruption platform. Whether his new broom will truly clean out the Augean stable of Mexican corruption is not yet clear. What has become clear, however, is that dicey drug-related money will find willing takers in nations where the rule of law takes a back seat to the greed of a small, self-serving elite. Until recently, both the World Bank and the IMF regularly failed to comment on such sources of liquidity, as if no comment from them made the problem irrelevant. Private bank secrecy also magnified the problem.

The Mexican experience was repeated in varying degrees in Thailand, the Philippines, Malaysia and Indonesia. This was in large part due to the continued loss of confidence in the transparency and accountability of public sector management. In Malaysia, despite the Prime Minister's pious rantings against 'foreign speculators', it was mainly local businessmen who were cashing in and looking for shelter offshore. This exodus amounted to a vote of no confidence in Malaysia's leadership. The IMF and other creditors are now tightening their conditions on lending support to ASEAN (Association of South East Asian Nations) nations.

When India celebrated the 50th anniversary of its independence, its future remained somewhat cloudy. Alternately referred to as the 'world's largest democracy' or 'the world's largest kleptocracy', this is the nation whose founding pilgrim, Mahatma Gandhi, addressing a prayer meeting on 26 January 1948, just days before his martyrdom, expressed his deep concern about 'the demon of corruption'. He told his followers that 'indifference in such matters is criminal'. India has continued to struggle with corruption in public life. On 14 August 1997, India's President K. R. Narayanan expressed concern that India's greatest challenge now arises from the weakening of the moral and spiritual fibre in its public life. The evils of communalism, casteism, violence and especially corruption bedevil Indian society today. India's Prime Minister urged all Indians of every caste and creed to expose corruption at all levels in society, even if that meant Cabinet ministers or higher. During 2000, the Indian government issued indictments against a powerful Swiss- and UK-based Indian family for their alleged involvement in the Bofors arms scandal. As the suppliers of the funding of the Faith Zone in the ill-fated Dome, the family chose to stay out of India and close to senior politicians and friends in the UK, though at the time of writing they had returned to India.

new initiatives

During the last years of the second millennium there was an explosion of comment and steps to correct the pervasiveness of corruption. In the area of corporate bribery, international executives interviewed by the World Bank named corruption as the biggest obstacle to doing business in Latin America, the Caribbean and sub-Saharan Africa. Recently, a spokesman for a large German company, frequently tainted by bribery allegations, insisted that it now makes commercial sense to end corruption. This is understandable when Mr 10 per cent has become Mr 30 per cent in many emerging nations that are in need of vast investment in infrastructure and large-scale agricultural, social sector and industrial projects.

In 1996 the Paris-based OECD, an association comprising the 29 leading industrial powers, announced steps to have all member states (representing some 70 per cent of cross-border trade) institute domestic legislation to criminalize the payment of bribes in international business transactions by May 1998. The view was that this national legislation should mimic the USA's FCPA, which has long been encouraged by successive US administrations, in an effort to level the international trading field. The target date was missed as many nations awaited the first move by other countries. One could feel sceptical about whether this initiative might be a reaction by the traditional 'northern' exporting nations to the accelerating loss of worldwide market share to 'south to south' trade. Many emerging nation exporters, investors and natural resource extractors seem to be less concerned about giving up 30 per cent or more of the 'action' to influential high officials in target markets in order to win contracts, concessions and monopoly positions. Major 'northern' investors or suppliers are increasingly feeling the pinch on the returns on their profit margins, resulting from giving ever-higher 'free rides' to corrupt officials in their traditional foreign markets.

However, in the competitive world of top banking, legal and accounting firms, the facts of today's business life make one pessimistic. To test the water recently I asked a senior director of a leading London merchant bank whether their highly regarded money managers would consider managing offshore wealth from secret sources in the emerging nations. He answered: 'We would be pleased to manage such money if it were properly introduced. We would manage it more professionally, cost-effectively and ethically [!] than most of our competitors.'

A 'proper introduction' meant the careful assurance by another leading bank or top law firm that XYZ Trust, or whatever name was given to such monies, was not derived from drug dealing, crime or in support of terrorist activities. Further up the paper trail associated with money laundering, such assurances might easily have been constructed. 'Due diligence', in a competitive neomercantilist world of money managers, often means getting the biggest slice possible of the ever-growing pool of 'sanitized' monies and often involves very little diligence despite increasingly pious declarations to the contrary from some leading bankers. For the OECD initiative to lead to enforceable action against corporate bribery, theft of national wealth and other sources of illicit money worldwide, all onshore and offshore bankers, lawyers, accountants and operators of national border-penetrating electronic money transfer systems will have to be conscripted into the battle.

There are a number of other international initiatives designed to combat corruption. The World Bank has tightened its guidelines on public procurement contracts. These now include provisions for sanctions on borrower countries and companies that engage in corrupt practices. The Bank has also started to withhold support from countries where the final beneficiaries from funding cannot be identified. The IMF's new emphasis on fighting corruption worldwide means that proposed lines of credit would be dependent on evidence of 'good governance'. Criteria could include emphasis on health and education, overhauling the tax system, improving court practices, strengthening private property rights and opening government ledgers to more frequent review.

All of these new initiatives are welcome and certainly overdue. They have been brought into clear focus particularly in the way in which the IMF and the World Bank have dealt with neighbouring Uganda and Kenya in recent years. These steps reflect those organizations' new resolve to address Lord Bauer's memorable concern that aid is a mechanism whereby poor people in rich countries are taxed to support the lifestyles of rich people in poor countries. Likewise, all of these initiatives address the admonition of the eighteenth-century statesman Edmund Burke that the only thing necessary for the triumph of evil is for good men to do nothing. Perhaps 2001 is indeed a banner year for the unbundling of the pernicious impact of 'Corruption Incorporated'. Time, and the work of the world's better men and women, will tell.

chapter 9

trade

Jennifer Potter

> Free trade is God's diplomacy and there is no other certain way of uniting people in the bonds of peace.
>
> Richard Cobden, 1857

introduction

Relationships based on trade have always been important within human society. Cultural and natural diversity around the regions of the world has meant that people have exchanged what they have in relative abundance for those things which they cannot produce or make but which are available from other places. The economist Ricardo formalized this into the theory of 'comparative advantage', and reference to this theory is a common point for those who advocate 'free trade'. However, arguments over 'free trade' on the one side and 'protectionism' on the other have swayed back and forth over the centuries. In almost all cases it has been the dominant forces of the day that have sought to direct trade according to their perceived interests. The creation of the European Community and its development into a fully fledged Union reveals the political benefits arising from the formation of a single market. Similarly, the US Helms-Burton Law sought to penalize all those countries that wished to trade with Cuba.

At the start of a new millennium, trade has come to be seen as a critical element in 'globalization' and has become an issue of public debate to a greater extent than, perhaps, at any time in history. The concept of trade has come to embrace ever-widening areas of concern. From being about the exchange of goods or commodities for other commodities or for money, it now embraces concerns such as competition policy, food safety, labelling, labour standards, environmental standards and intellectual property. Some of these issues have usually been subject to domestic jurisdiction but there is now a blurring between what is a domestic concern, and what is regional and international. Consumers have little realization of where their goods originate from or even where they have been assembled. There is little public understanding of the elaborate and detailed discussions that go on around the exchange of each type of traded item.

Previously trade was about goods – primary products from farming or mining mostly from less developed places and manufactured items from more developed places. Yet today we need to add the trade in services, made possible by rapid growth in information technology and the growth of English as an international lingua franca. National boundaries are porous. The regulation of trade and commerce, if it is to be effective, can no longer be done nationally. National problems require regional and international solutions.

In theory, reciprocal trade should work to the mutual benefit of all parties. We live in an era of exponentially growing trade in goods and services and yet there is a paradox and a challenge within it. Job insecurity has increased, there is pressure on wage levels and conditions of work, mergers and acquisitions hollow out entire industrial sectors in some countries or regions, prices for primary products fluctuate wildly within a downward trend and there is a growing gap both within and between countries. Despite the perceived benefits of globalization the gap between rich and poor is widening rather than narrowing. In addition, the over-exploitation of natural resources and the production of waste materials threaten the environmental sustainability and the quality of the planet's life. This issue, more than any other, demands a whole-earth response.

Trade is now central to the debate over how globalization can work to the benefit rather than the detriment of the world's poor. The World Trade Organization (WTO) has become a focus for protest and anger both for issues that are within its remit and for a whole swathe that are best dealt with in other international bodies, like the World Bank. The struggle for a humane future for the planet and its people is waged on many fronts but pre-eminently in the struggle within and between the Bretton Woods 'Triplets'.

the WTO
Seattle 1999 changed the relative obscurity of the WTO. The abortive attempt to launch a new and comprehensive trade liberalization round in Seattle brought the WTO to centre stage within a wider public debate about trade and the rules that govern it. For many people, Seattle was their first encounter with the WTO. Given this situation, a little background might be helpful in trying to understand the WTO as it is presently organized.

The WTO grew out of the General Agreement on Tariffs and Trade (GATT), which was part of the post-Second World War effort to secure peace and stability for the world, along with the United Nations, the World Bank and the International Monetary Fund (IMF). The original idea had been to set up an International Trade Organization (ITO) as one of the pillars of the UN (an idea that has returned as part of the proposals for reforming the WTO), but this idea was rejected by the United States. Interestingly, the original ITO Charter included issues such as monopolies, restrictive business practices in general and measures to address employment and worker rights. Thus part of today's agenda around corporate accountability was already under discussion 50 years ago. So GATT became a curious institutional creature, meeting for periodic trade negotiations but deprived of a permanent secretariat that could act as a continuous regulating authority. There were seven of these trade rounds before the final Uruguay Round (1986–93), which more or less stumbled into establishing the World Trade Organization.

GATT – many of whose provisions and procedures were carried over into the WTO – was very much a child of its time. Its creation mirrored the geopolitical structure that emerged following the end of the Second World War, and, not surprisingly, this was reflected in its agenda. The disastrous effects of the Depression, with its downward spiral of retaliatory protectionism, were seen to have been a major contributory factor to the outbreak of the Second World War, and as a result GATT's focus was on lowering existing high tariff barriers. In 1947, when 23 nations signed GATT, the process of decolonization had scarcely begun – there was little challenge to the fact that a small clique of powerful nations laid down the rules for 'world trade'. By the time the Uruguay Round was complete and the WTO was officially established in January 1995 there were 115 signatories, and the number of member countries continues to rise (140 at the last count, in 2000). In the intervening time the pattern of world trade has developed a size and complexity far beyond that envisaged by the original GATT.

Membership of the WTO entails a commitment to 29 individual legal texts, 25 Ministerial declarations and understandings and 24,000 pages of country schedules on such detailed matters as bound tariff concessions, domestic and export subsidy reduction commitments and initial pledges to open up services. All the Uruguay Round accords were rolled up into a 'single undertaking' – obligations which had been developed during the GATT years without the participation of any of the new members but which now required implementation within a set period. Many developing countries signed the Marrakesh Agreement (which concluded the Uruguay Round) with insufficient appreciation of its details and inadequate capacity to implement all of its elements within the agreed time frame. One of the major tasks facing the WTO is to work out a realistic timescale and procedures for implementation, but on a basis that is responsive to members' varying economic situations. The developing countries also expected major changes in the protectionist practices of industrialized countries that have yet to materialize.

On paper the WTO commits its members to certain basic principles. The principle of non-discrimination states that when any trading partner agrees a tariff cut it is extended, without further negotiation, to all other WTO members. In theory at least, this means that smaller countries should reap the benefits of more accessible trading without having to involve themselves in costly negotiations. Members of the WTO also commit themselves to progressive market liberalization without any 'backsliding' towards unilaterally raising tariffs on any items on which they have already been reduced. Through the Generalized System of Preferences there is recognition that the poorest and least developed nations need positive discrimination. In practice, however, this recognition on its own is inadequate.

As with its GATT predecessor, decision-making in the WTO is via consensus. The danger – as illustrated by Seattle – is that the process is unwieldy and inefficient. In part the problem is the result of the significant expansion in membership that has occurred over the years. Each member country has one vote and there is no veto mechanism built into the procedure. Unlike its predecessor, which had no competence to enforce agreements, the WTO does have 'teeth' in the form of a Disputes Settlement Body. This body can set up a panel to adjudicate cases of alleged infringement of the WTO rules and sanction fines or retaliation towards countries found to be guilty of such infringement. Interestingly, the first Disputes Settlement process found against the USA in a case brought by Venezuela and Brazil. The USA was found to have set lower standards for domestically produced petrol products than it required of imported products. However, it does not take much to realize that small economies have few possibilities of effective 'retaliation' against big economies such as that of the USA.

Before analysing the WTO's future and the prospects for a new round of negotiations, it may be helpful to assess the organization's operation on its own terms. For instance, to what extent is the WTO a 'world' organization, or is it just a means for the main trading nations – the 'Quad' (the USA, Canada, the EU and Japan) in particular and the OECD in general – to gain additional market access? Some 80 per cent of world trade is between the main industrialized and developed nations. Some commentators have referred to the IMF, the World Bank and the WTO as the 'trinity of the market', an Anglo-American search for world order based on their own interests. Further questions can be raised about the extent to which the WTO is concerned with enhancing trade, and especially 'free trade'. Closer examination of the WTO reveals that the word 'free' is chameleon-like, changing according to political expediency and specific circumstances. Most industrialized countries are interested in trading 'services' freely around the world but are less interested in free trade in labour into their domestic economies. It is well known that EU countries are very reluctant to open up their markets to agricultural produce from the developing world and that the Common Agricultural Policy (CAP) gives enormous subsidies to European farmers.

Some economists, notably Jagdish Bhagwati of Columbia University, point up a current irony in the 'free trade' debate.[1] In the 1950s and 1960s, when developed countries were optimistic about the rewards to be reaped by dismantling trade barriers, developing countries were cautious and largely sceptical about the benefits of integrating into the world economy. 'Free trade' was seen as a form of neo-colonialism. However, by the 1990s, he suggests, the roles had reversed. The developing countries increasingly saw integration into the world economy as an opportunity, while developed countries were beginning to fear that the existence of abundant cheap labour in the South would threaten both jobs and wage levels in their own countries. Bhagwati maintains that these fears are largely unjustified, but it is noteworthy that it was the US unions that provided the largest number of street protestors in Seattle.

the WTO post-Seattle

So what are the prospects for a new round of trade negotiations? To be able to assess those prospects there needs to be some understanding of why the Millennium Round failed. There is little consensus as to why the Seattle trade round failed, but the following are some of the explanations that have been offered. To many commentators the United States was deficient in its organization of the event. Divisions over who would succeed Ruggiero as Director-General wasted significant time. In addition, it became increasingly evident that the traditional procedures for reaching consensus were inadequate to deal with the number and diversity of the member nations represented in Seattle. Journalists noted that developed nations acted as if it was 1949, not 1999, and continued with the in-group 'Green Room' procedure, which effectively excluded most developing countries from keeping up with the process. In many ways, however, this conflict was symptomatic of a wider struggle between developing and developed countries as to who makes the rules that determine world trade. Developing Southern countries complained that the developed North had failed to open up its markets, especially in agricultural goods and textiles, as they had committed themselves to do, and that the North was, moreover, adding non-tariff barriers to keep produce and goods out.

Should there even be a new round?[2] Wouldn't it be preferable to rewind the script to the pre-WTO days? That is not desirable even if it were possible. There is no way to roll back 50 years of increasing global integration. Information technology and new forms of communication mean that we live interconnected lives in interdependent economies. The placard messages of Seattle cried 'Kill the WTO', but the majority of governments around the world agree that some sort of rules-based trade system is necessary. If the WTO were scrapped, it is possible that dominant economic powers like the United States would use their muscle even more ruthlessly against the vulnerable of the world – the textile industry in Bangladesh, for example. There would be a proliferation of bilateral arrangements, which would make it infinitely more difficult to tackle environmental or labour issues.

The WTO or some regulatory body needs to exist, but what exists at present demands reform. Developing countries need to be able to air their concerns and know that they are being taken seriously. This will mean the developed world making some serious movement on meeting its commitments to allow greater access for primary and manufactured products from the developing world. For the European Union, it will mean looking far more seriously at the impacts of the CAP with its huge built-in subsidies, which are unsustainable as the Union enlarges eastwards into more agriculturally based economies.

The WTO's decision-making process also needs attention, especially given the emergence of regional trading blocs like the North American Free Trade Association (NAFTA), the Association of South East Asian Nations (ASEAN) and the European Union. WTO trade agreements is one of those areas, for example, where the European Commission negotiates on behalf of its members. This means that there has to be a complicated and often fraught process of consensus building within the EU before discussing matters at the WTO. At the recent Nice Summit the competence of the Commission to negotiate trade issues was further extended. It is still unclear whether this will complicate or simplify the process.

The diversity of interests and the difficulty of arriving at a consensus within the EU has been graphically illustrated very recently during the protracted negotiation of a Free Trade Agreement between the EU and South Africa. Far from being a vehicle for helping a newly democratized South Africa enter the global economy, this was a bitterly fought battle over port and sherry and latterly over ouzo and grappa. Significantly, these are items that South Africa produces in insignificant amounts. The negotiations were really aimed at bringing South Africa within EU trading priorities – introducing reciprocity into the relationship but excluding those product areas where South Africa is competitive with EU member states. There was no commitment from the EU to cease the 'dumping' of surpluses of subsidized products such as sugar onto the South African market in such a way that not only sugar grow-ing but also sugar-based industries such as confectionery and tinned fruit are undermined. These negotiations showed clearly the gulf between the supportive rhetoric and the harsh realities of the actual negotiating process.

The negotiation of Free Trade Areas, such as that recently concluded by the EU with South Africa, is a prototype of how the EU hopes to proceed in its relations with the African, Caribbean and Pacific countries in future. Currently there is a proliferation of these agreements all around the world. As a result it is now questionable whether 'regionalism' is adding to or detracting from the global multilateral free trade agenda. There are signs that these arrangements are in danger of becoming protectionist trading blocs. If these trends continue then there is a danger that regionalism might inhibit moves towards a more open and transparent global trading system.

Space does not permit a detailed examination of environmental or labour issues as related to the WTO. Much is written, not least in the latest White Paper from the Department for International Development, about countries moving towards sustainable patterns of consumption and production, but there are scarcely any hard proposals about how that virtuous state might be brought about.[3] Global economic growth on a business-as-usual basis is unsustainable. Moving nations and companies to grapple with the implica-tions of this is perhaps the greatest global challenge. There has been some welcome movement in this direction in some countries in the form of Codes of Conduct, the Ethical Trading Initiative and the Guidelines for Multinational

Enterprises of the OECD, which now need to be broadened and strengthened.

While trade does contribute to many environmental problems like forest destruction or the export of toxic waste, it also has the potential to contribute environmental benefits through applying market mechanisms to costs that are currently not factored in and through removing distortions and restrictions that produce environmental degradation. In this, as in all other areas, political will to tackle these issues is the critical factor. For environmental concerns to be taken more seriously on the world stage there needs to be a comprehensive 'environmental body' capable of coordinating all the agreements that are scattered around the multilateral firmament.

the way ahead

There will need to be much greater assistance given to small nations to attend WTO meetings and committees and to establish missions in Geneva. An advisory centre funded by some of the developed nations, including the UK, has now been set up. This is a positive step, but if it is to be truly effective it will need additional resources. The USA had more lawyers in Seattle than all the developing nations have put together. The playing field will never be level but there must be greater fairness. There will also need to be reform of the processes of the WTO so those things can get done. Some commentators have suggested that there should be a UN-like body of permanent members, but that in itself would be an extremely contentious proposal. There will also need to be more openness about the working of the WTO and its Disputes Settlement Body. Some progress has been made by making information available on the Internet, but much more needs to be known about the influence of external lobby groups on the panels in the Disputes procedure. The recent failure of the WTO to allow a group of non-governmental organizations to file an *amicus curiae* (friend at court) submission on the case between France and Canada over asbestos, after initially seeming to welcome it, is a disturbing development.

The way is ahead and not back. 'Globalization', in terms of the shrinkage in time and space that our world has experienced over the last decades, is here to stay. There is no escape from it. It is a fact of life – we may like it or hate it, but we have to come to terms with its implications. How we run our economy in a globalized world is a matter of human priority and choice. The world economy, with trade as one component of it, is not an end in itself but a means to an end. There is an alternative because people and institutions were responsible for making the world economy what it is now and people and institutions can be responsible for taking it in another direction, in which human development and welfare rather than economic growth and gross domestic product are the benchmark. Both governments and multinational corporations have an interest in the long-term development of a stable, equitable, people-focused global economy.

There will always be painful economic adjustments to be made within countries and between countries and politicians who have been responsible for signing up to international agreements. We need to stop using bodies like the EU or the WTO as scapegoats when tough decisions need to be taken and implemented. There is a need to recognize, both nationally and internationally, that there will always be short-term dislocations produced by the changing economic landscape. Governments and international organizations need to work on providing adequate safety nets for those hardest hit by such dislocations and on equipping people with new skills for future employment.

Just as it has been possible to make globalization work for the rich, so it is possible to make it work for the poor. At the international level this will demand a vision of a world which has to provide a humane life for all if it is to survive.[4] At the national level this demands a willingness to ensure that the benefits of trade and all other forms of economic activity reach the whole and not just part of society. The alternative is a world of political instability and lawlessness, of trafficking in people, and of ever more sophisticated and lucrative international crime outstripping legitimate trade. There are few signs of this vision for a humane future or of a political will to work towards it in the nations of the world. The Church and other faith communities have an important responsibility for holding up such a vision to the world.

chapter 10
global institutions
Claire Melamed

introduction

The increased speed and volume of movements of money, ideas, goods and people around the world has thrown up new challenges for politicians and policy makers. Though the main concern of national governments is still what happens within their borders, they are no longer able to meet their national objectives without cooperation with other governments. Armed conflicts can spread across borders, environmental disasters are not respecters of political boundaries, and international criminals are devising new and ever more inventive ways of evading national controls.

There is a range of national problems that can only be solved internationally. In addition, actions at the national level increasingly impinge upon the governments and people of other countries. When the European Union attempts to control imports of textiles to protect jobs in Europe, this has consequences for workers in Africa and Asia. If a country in Africa imposes environmental conditions on investment, companies and jobs in the UK might be affected.

One response to the growing international dimension to national policy has been a huge increase in the number of global institutions. At the beginning of the twentieth century, there were around 30 intergovernmental organizations. By the beginning of the new millennium, this number had swelled to over 250.[1] There is also an ever-increasing number of international treaties and agreements on common goals, such as the International Development Targets agreed at a series of international conferences between 1990 and 1995, and the Kyoto Protocol on greenhouse gas emissions, agreed in 1999. However, some of these agreements and organizations have at times been seen as part of the problems thrown up by globalization, rather than as part of the solution.

Though there is agreement among most countries that they need to cooperate to resolve common problems, the terms and scope of that cooperation are far from agreed. As well as governments, a range of different groups including non-government organizations, Church groups and trade unions have become involved in the debate around the proper structure and role of global institutions. Two issues are key to the new dilemmas. First, there is the problem of participation. Who makes the rules in global institutions, and in whose interests those rules operate, are increasingly fraught questions, which have been debated in public on the streets of Seattle and Prague as well as in the corridors of the World Bank and the World Trade Organization (WTO). Second, the aims and objectives of global institutions are increasingly coming under discussion. Is the aim of these institutions to make the economy work better, through the pursuit of 'stability' or 'free trade', or should global institutions try to make the economy work differently, in order to resolve global problems such as poverty and inequality?

a history of global institutions

The existing system of global institutions was established at the end of the Second World War. The foundations for the World Bank and the IMF were laid at the Bretton Woods conference in 1944, where the victorious powers in the war gathered to discuss how to manage the post-war world. The IMF was charged with stabilizing global exchange rates and assisting countries with short-term liquidity problems. The World Bank was responsible for longer-term projects, channelling public and (mainly) private sector investment. Though an International Trade Organization was part of the original plan at Bretton Woods, objections coming mainly from the USA meant that it was not established with the other two institutions. It was not until 1995 that the WTO was established.

The international institutions created at the end of the Second World War find themselves, at the beginning of the twenty-first century, operating in quite a different political climate. There are over three times as many states in the world now as there were in 1945. The new states are mainly the ex-colonies of European powers, many of them countries with very low average incomes. The influx of new countries into the global political system has heightened the debate around participation in global institutions, and driven new issues such as the pressing problems of global poverty and inequality higher up the political agenda.

Economic, as well as political, structures have changed. There are companies that are bigger than most states (half of the 100 biggest economies in the world are companies rather than countries). The speed, volume and value of economic activity have changed dramatically. Governments do much more, as they manage increasingly complex welfare systems and attempt to balance more and more competing interests, and much less, as their control over the companies within their borders is whittled away through liberalization. Growing economic interdependence has made it more impor-tant that countries cooperate through global institutions, but it has also raised the stakes in economic cooperation.

The system that we have now has three different components. Some global institutions, like the WTO, are forums for governments to reach agreements that commit them to certain domestic policies. Governments jointly agree that each will, individually, reduce tariffs on certain goods or allow certain types of investment. The domestic policies of some governments are also affected by the operations of the more interventionist agencies, which actively involve themselves in the running of national economies through their role as arbiters of debt relief programmes or through provision of support in times of financial crisis. Finally, individual governments also make agreements on specific goals, such as reducing the level of green-house gas emissions, or protecting human rights, or reducing the numbers of people in poverty.

Different governments have very different relationships to these three types of global activity. Generally, the governments of industrialized countries tend to be most affected by the first and the third components, while those of developing countries are most affected by the more interventionist agencies (with a few exceptions, such as the 1976 UK government's appeal to the IMF for support following a collapse in the value of the pound and balance of payments problems. The IMF demanded cuts in spending and tax increases as conditions for the loan).

The increased number and diversity of institutions, as well as changes in the nature of the challenges they face, has put ever-increasing pressure on this system of global institutions. This pressure was evident on the streets of Seattle and Prague in 1999, as well as in the governments of developing countries and the meeting rooms of the IMF, the World Bank and the WTO themselves. The pressure has come from two sources: concern over the level and scope of participation in international institutions, and concern over the goals of global economic management.

participation

As more countries have begun to participate in global institutions, so questions of participation have become ever more important to the functioning of these institutions. Of the existing international institutions (the IMF, the World Bank, the UN and the WTO), some are more democratic than others. The IMF and the World Bank are probably the least democratic. The original Bretton Woods structure was established by relatively few countries, and the existing structure still reflects the interests and concerns of the founders. Seven countries (the USA, UK, Germany, France, Japan, Italy and Canada) control nearly half of the votes at the World Bank. The USA holds nearly 20 per cent of the total votes in the IMF.

The IMF and the World Bank are probably the institutions that, through the conditions they impose on the support they provide, have the greatest impact on the economies of the poorest countries in the world. However, they are also the institutions in which these countries are the least represented. In practice, a few countries dominate decision-making in the IMF and the World Bank, and they can often impose quite specific conditions on the economies of other countries. In the process of negotiating rescue packages for East Asian countries hit by the 1997 financial crisis, there was often an uncanny similarity between the final package and US interests in the region. For example, in the package negotiated for South Korea, one condition for receiving bailout funds was that the Korean government must open up the economy to imported auto parts. This had very little to do with the balance of payments problems that the package was supposedly dealing with, but it had been a constant demand of US trade negotiators in bilateral trade talks with South Korea for much of the 1990s. One negotiator claimed that the USA had achieved more in the six months of talks between South Korea and the IMF following the crisis than they had in ten years of bilateral negotiations.[2]

It is a similar story with debt relief. When debt relief packages for individual countries are being discussed, debtor country governments are not always able to get hold of the documents sent to the World Bank's board. Government representatives of debtor countries are not there when the final decisions are made on a country's eligibility for debt relief or on the conditions under which that relief will be granted.

The IMF and the World Bank have come under increasing criticism in the last few years, and the lack of democracy in their operations has been a major target of attack. Insiders and outsiders have argued that the institutions' lack of transparency and accountability are not only a bad basis for establishing a system of global governance based on participation and ownership by all countries, but also lead to bad policy. Conditions imposed on countries seeking debt relief, and on countries needing support following financial crisis, have, in many cases, increased the hardship suffered by the most vulnerable in those countries rather than improved the situation.

Though other institutions do not suffer from the same inbuilt lack of democracy as the World Bank and the IMF, they still reflect prevailing realities in the world rather than compensate for them. The WTO is supposedly based on a highly democratic system of one member one vote and decision-making by consensus. However, developing country members lack the capacity to participate effectively in the range of negotiations, disputes and reviews that are going on all the time in the WTO. The most important decisions are made informally by a small group of the major powers, with the formal meetings acting, in the words of one delegate, as a 'rubber stamp'.

One important difference between the Bretton Woods institutions and the WTO is that though the equality between countries in the WTO may exist only on paper, it does sometimes allow smaller countries to act together to prevent decisions being taken that they do not agree with. The failure to launch a new round of trade talks at the WTO meeting in Seattle in November 1999 was mainly due to the perception by many of the developing country government representatives that they were not fairly represented in the WTO, and were being excluded from most of the important decisions taken there. As a group of African trade ministers said on the last day of the conference: 'There is no transparency in the proceedings and African countries are being marginalized and generally excluded on issues of vital importance for our peoples and their future.'[3]

The contrasting structures and experiences of the Bretton Woods institutions and the WTO show that, though more democratic structures are essential for the proper functioning of global institutions, they are not enough. The WTO is, on paper, very much more democratic than the IMF or the World Bank. However, when countries start off from such an unequal basis, more than a level playing field is required to give all countries an equal chance in global institutions. The experience of the WTO shows that the structures of global institutions need to be designed with the capacity of the weakest members in mind, so that all are able to participate.

means and ends

An interesting conflict is emerging in global governance. It is a conflict that some like to pretend does not exist, while others see it as the major problem of global institutions in the new century. The problem is one of means and ends. Governments make some agreements on final objectives, such as reducing poverty, and others on common means, such as freer trade. However, in some cases means and ends contradict each other. For example, on trade it is now recognized by most academic commentators that trade liberalization, though it may contribute to poverty reduction in some cases, can also contribute to poverty in others. Signing up to commitments to reduce poverty may actually contradict making commitments to liberalize trade in particular sectors.

The conflict between means and ends has also been an issue in the negotiations on debt relief. For the World Bank and the IMF, the issue is debt sustainability. The aim is to reduce the debt to a level that can actually be paid back, and to put in place policies that will generate growth, enabling countries to pay back debt faster and with less cost to their economies. Agencies such as Christian Aid and CAFOD have continually said that the aim of debt relief should not be to reduce debt to the maximum amount that can feasibly be paid, but to reduce debt to the extent that the payment of debt does not jeopardize human development and poverty reduction. It may be possible for a country to pay back a certain level of debt, but this may be at the cost of health and education services or public investment.[4]

The creation of the WTO has exacerbated these problems with coherence among global institutions. Agreements in the WTO on specific changes in national policy are unique in being enforceable through trade sanctions. Other international agreements on common goals rely on goodwill and political pressure for their enforcement by individual governments. This has meant that, in practice, agreements made in the WTO have tended to override other international agreements – in effect, the means have started to override the ends.

According to the WTO, its mission is to help trade flow 'smoothly, freely, fairly and predictably'. However, this does not indicate anything about whether free trade can help governments to meet the goals they have committed themselves to in international agreements. In many cases, the answer may be no.

For example, the mere threat of WTO action (brandished by an infant formula company) persuaded the Guatemalan government to backtrack on its compliance with the World Health Organization ruling on breast milk substitutes in 1995. In effect, in order to abide by agreements on free trade the Guatemalan government had to compromise on its support for international agreements to promote child health. Trade agreements may also, under some circumstances, contradict poverty reduction goals. In the Philippines Christian Aid's partner organization, the Ibon Foundation, has documented how trade liberalization under structural adjustment has led to huge dislocation in the sugar sector. Following increases in sugar imports after trade liberalization, domestic producers are suffering a fall in demand for their crop. Ibon says the costs will fall hardest on the poorest. The 413,000 farm workers who could be dislocated already suffer from food insecurity and lack the capital and education to shift very easily to other forms of work. For them the future looks bleak.

It is worth remembering that no government in history has ever managed to reduce poverty significantly through liberalization alone. The most dramatic reductions in poverty in the twentieth century, in the newly industrializing economies of East Asia, or in China, all came about through careful management of trade and investment, designed to build up competitive local industries.

The creation of the WTO has highlighted a problem in global institutions that was already clear in the operation of the World Bank and the IMF and the conditions attached to debt relief and the granting of loans. There is an increasing danger that, in the global economic system, means are being elevated over ends. Organizations like Christian Aid and CAFOD argue that the point is not whether trade is 'free', or whether a particular country has liberalized its capital account, or whether government expenditure stays below a certain level, but what contribution all these instruments can make to the internationally agreed goals of reducing poverty and protecting the environment and human rights.[5] In some cases these instruments might help governments to achieve these ends. In others they won't.

conclusion

The major global institutions suffer from the same problems. Created in the image of existing power relationships in the international system, they are dominated by the interests of a few powerful states. The majority of the world's countries have little or no voice within the system, yet they are affected by the rules made and the policies promoted by the global institutions. Public disquiet with the system is increasing with the perception that it is working for the interests of a few global corporations, and against the wishes of the majority of the world's population. Their structure, and the dominance of particular countries within them, means that they take a particular approach to their role and to the problems of global economic governance, one often based around means (like trade liberalization) rather than ends (like poverty reduction). The net result is that countries are required to use the same policy instruments (financial liberalization, trade liberalization, privatization, etc.), with very different results: in some cases poverty may be reduced, but elsewhere it may be increased.

What is needed is a reversal of this situation. Instead of common instruments, we need global institutions to work towards common ends (poverty reduction, environmental sustainability and human rights protection) and to provide the flexibility and security for governments to agree on what might be quite different instruments for achieving these ends. Liberalization might be what is required in some countries, while in others domestic industries might need to be protected from foreign competitors.

For poverty reduction worldwide to be combined with financial stability and growth, global institutions need to become more flexible in their approach to solving economic problems. The major lesson of the experiences with debt relief and structural adjustment should be that, in economic policy as in footwear, one size does not fit all. Global institutions should not attempt to impose a single model of economic management. Instead, they should provide the space and the security for countries to decide together how to resolve the many and varied problems that have a global dimension. There may be many solutions to poverty, to environmental degradation and to human rights abuses, but all are more achievable if they are backed up by a system of global institutions that is genuinely participative, based around commonly agreed objectives, and flexible in what is needed to achieve those objectives.

part III
meeting the challenge

chapter 11

the silent word still speaks

globalization and the interpretation of Scripture

Peter Selby

introduction

This chapter began life with an invitation to present to a seminar on the interpretation of Scripture a case study, a worked example that might anchor the topic of the interpretation of Scripture by testing it on a major contemporary issue[1]. So this is not an attempt at an essay on the current state of the global market and how it operates, let alone a gaze into a crystal ball to discern how it is going to operate; for that the reader should look at other chapters. My perspective on it is probably not so very different from that of many non-economists who might be reading this. It is written on the assumption that my readers and I share a view of ourselves as more or less adequately informed observers of a vast, powerful and mysterious reality (I shall be returning to those words later) with which we all have a sense of coming to terms, but of which none of us feels in any sense in charge.

I shall seek to treat 'globalization', or the 'global market', as a case study in scriptural interpretation, as a phenomenon focusing our minds on how Scripture is to be interpreted. And that in turn provokes another preliminary observation. It is recorded that when the New Testament scholar Christopher Evans was presented with his *Festschrift* entitled *What about the New Testament? Essays in Honour of C. F. Evans*, Eric Mascall was heard to remark, no doubt only partly in jest, that a more appropriate book would have been entitled *What about C. F. Evans? Essays in Honour of the New Testament*. That piece of academic banter becomes a rather serious matter when it comes to a subject like globalization. After all, making the global market a case study in biblical interpretation could imply that the adequacy of a method of interpreting Scripture is to be judged by the extent to which it can take account of the phenomenon of globalization. Would it not be truer to what Christians have believed about the Scriptures to say that the adequacy of the global market is to be judged by how far it accords with our understanding of Scripture? If the global market cannot be integrated into the ways we think it right to interpret Scripture, isn't it so much the worse for the global market?

What I am highlighting here is a struggle in which we find ourselves engaged between two positions. The first would say that our experience is to be interpreted in the light of the revealed word of God (let us call that a 'conservative' position). The second would say that the word of God is to be understood and interpreted in the light of our experience (let us call that a 'liberal' position). When you put the issue in that way an immediate difficulty appears: the first position, the 'conservative' one, seems to me to be the only one that can be theologically defended, while the latter seems to be the only one that is practically possible. On the one hand, to be claimed by the belief that the word of God has been revealed means seeking to measure all you experience, all you are and all you do by it. On the other hand, whenever we seek to express what the word of God means for now we seem to be basing our understanding on our own thought forms and perceptions, and that seems to be true even, perhaps even especially, of those who would most vehemently deny that they are doing so.

how does 'the globalization of the market economy' send you to the Scriptures?

The fact that we would not find it easy to say 'so much the worse for the global market' alerts us to the most important feature of it that I perceive, and that is that we experience it as something about which we have no choice. So we instinctively accept the words of the report of Section 2 of the 1998 Lambeth Conference:

> Since the last Lambeth Conference, the greatest single new force shaping the world in which we do mission is the globalisation of the market economy. This is bringing rapid change. The groups most affected by these changes yet least equipped to deal with them are our children and young people. They live in a world where nothing is certain. They are offered only opinions, not truth. Among the most visible effects of this globalisation is the flight to the cities of people absorbed into the market culture.[2]

The report of that section goes on to link globalization with the rise of nationalism and other signs of the fragmentation of national and cultural identities. In this and other ways, the report of Section 2 of the Lambeth Conference, *Called to Live and Proclaim the Good News*, reflects a point of view that it is barely possible for us to imagine contesting: the world described by the word 'globalization' is the world we inhabit. The globalization of the market economy, we instinctively believe, constitutes the inescapable context of human living at the turn of the millennium.

I propose to select some of the most prominent features of globalization and see how we may address them from Scripture. That is the study of the case; then I shall see what that has to say about the fundamental issue of biblical interpretation.

The words just quoted from Section 2 of Lambeth 1998 imply, I believe very accurately, a link between the global market and what we have come to know as a postmodern world view. We are told we are in a situation of the end of the 'grand narrative' or overarching world view. There is no longer any prospect of a winner in the contest of total world views. We are instead in a marketplace of ideas in which picking and mixing is all there is to do: all is opinion; where is truth? You may believe you are claimed by the word of God revealed; but the very air you breathe tells you what you are actually doing is making a Christian choice among many religious possibilities, and a religious choice among many possible world views. You have no choice but to make choices; and the world that emerges from the choices we all make – and above all are prepared to pay for – is the only world there is. The end of the grand narrative turns out actually to be the triumph of the global market as the grand narrative in which you are offered a bit part, and it is an offer you cannot refuse.

Immediately as I contemplate this, biblical moments rush to the surface of my mind. The pride of the construction of Babel and the scattering of human communities unable any more to communicate; the Pentecostal reversal that seems to offer unity in the gospel while diversity remains and in which all can hear the word of God 'in their own language'. Talk of the global market recalls Luke's characterization of the Athenians' interest in every novelty, something he describes as a captivity from which only the making known of the unknown God could release them. It reminds me also of the pagan culture of Corinth of which the apostle Paul is so stern a critic. Above all, perhaps surprisingly, I find myself reflecting on the demons of Gadara, so many that Legion was their name. Is this multiplex economy of commodity and idea, of narrative and possibility, actually a kind of possession from which Christ offers the only release, and is it only a coincidence that the release of their captive was only purchased at the cost of somebody's livelihood?

But multiplexity is only one of the features of the globalized market economy. There are others implicit in the fact of globalization itself. The range and speed with which it is now possible to engage with one another around the globe brings to the mind all that the Scriptures say about the global character of God's project, the universality of the divine ambition. It is hard not to feel the excitement of global communication as echoing in some sense the desire of a God for whom it is too light a thing to restore the exiles of Israel to their homeland, the triumphant conclusion of the Lucan narrative of the gospel's progress to the heart of the empire and the final cosmic glorification of the Lamb. God's purpose is global – in fact universal. Francis Watson's words in *Text, Church and World* make this point:

> If the triune God brings the world into being for its own sake but above all for the sake of human beings, made in his likeness to engage in dialogue with him, then this beginning must determine the theme and the scope of the story that follows. . . . [A] book which begins with the assertion that 'In the beginning God created the heavens and the earth' establishes, through the comprehensiveness of its scope, the expectation that the narrative will lead eventually to an equally comprehensive goal – as indeed it does, in the creation of new heavens and a new earth at the close of the book of Revelation. The universal horizons of this narrative do not permit the extraction of 'the story of Jesus' to serve as the legitimation-myth of a small community in its self-imposed exile from the world.[3]

If the sheer multiplexity of the world enabled by a globalized market sent me back to find in the Scriptures some rather negative, critical reflections, globalization itself carries sufficient echoes of the divine purpose to invite real celebration. What the Lord said about hypocrisy seems to leap off the page as a description of the way in which the portable radio sealed the fate of the Shah of Iran and the ubiquitous television doomed the Berlin Wall: 'There is nothing covered up that will not be uncovered, nothing hidden that will not be made known.'[4] Human rights conventions play their part in changing people's minds about issues such as data protection; but it is events that change behaviour, and the essential uncontrollability of information is the reality with which we have to come to terms. The Lord may have been talking about hypocrisy, but it seems as though he might just as easily have been talking about my filing cabinet when he continues: 'You may take it, then, that everything you have said in the dark will be heard in broad daylight, and what you have whispered behind closed doors will be shouted from the housetops.'

It was the issue of debt, both domestic and international, that most recently drove me into the Scriptures with new eyes, causing me to find there a range of economic concerns that somehow had passed me by. There is no doubt that the Jubilee 2000 campaign, whatever it may or may not have achieved for the poorest nations of the earth, and whatever people may have learned from it about the situation of indebted nations, was an incredibly successful piece of biblical teaching. There are people who knew a great deal about the Bible without having the Sabbath and Jubilee legislation anywhere near the top of their consciousness; there are, I suspect, now quite a number of people who still know very little about the Bible but who are aware that it says something about cancelling debt.

The debt crisis, and the credit and debt economy generally, are unavoidable outcomes of the globalization of the market economy. The question of what the Bible has to offer to this matter in reality is profoundly significant (I remember being more than slightly alarmed when my archbishop fixed me with a penetrating gaze and asked, 'Are you a jubilee fundamentalist?' He seemed to be pleased when I said that I wasn't!). This question goes to the heart of the matter: what happens when you take a difficult question to the Bible? To quote the title of John Goldingay's immensely illuminating book, which will be the models of Scripture that you will deploy?[5] Heated scholarly debate about whether jubilees ever happened always seemed to tell me rather more about the politics of the exegetes than the history of the matter.

Two things are clear to me: the anti-avoidance legislation contained in the jubilee texts suggests that even if no jubilee ever happened some mean creditors at least thought they might. And second, had the Jubilee/Sabbath system ever really taken hold in Hebrew or later Jewish society the Jubilee prophecy could not have been used by Christ in that now liturgically rather over-used passage in Luke 4 as a description of himself. When Our Lord uses the Jubilee prophecy as a pointer to himself he is not unhinging the notion of Jubilee from the economy, but rather radicalizing it far beyond what we may assume were the intentions of the original regulations.

What I mean is this: if you take to the Bible the difficult question of remitting unrepayable debt, or another difficult question like whether water companies should have the right to disconnect for non-payment, it will not be long before somebody proposes that the Levitical restriction on people retaining a person's only night covering as security for a loan settles the question. Where the servicing of debt places lives in danger the debt must be remitted; and in no circumstances should disconnection of water supplies for non-payment be allowed. I happen to agree with both those political judgements, but not because there's a text I can lift out of the Bible. What I get from a scriptural investigation of this issue is the doctrine that debt shall not have the last word in the human community and that Christ lived and died and rose again in order to establish precisely that. That doctrine is indeed one before which the globalized world economy needs to tremble, not just the water companies or the World Bank.

For it is becoming increasingly clear that the globalization of world markets is rooted in a particular view of the mechanism of exchange, namely money, which moves in rapidly increasing quantity at rapidly increasing speed, all of it representing increasing claims on the world's resources, all of it, that is to say, constituting further and further debt.[6] The aspects of globalization worth celebrating seem all to be compounded with the constantly increasing power of money in our lives. It is now money that travels the fastest and has the greatest capacity to make national boundaries obsolete and the democratic institutions by which we expect our lives to be regulated to become increasingly powerless.

Such discoveries sent me back to Scripture again, only to find there a far greater awareness of the importance and character of money than I had previously allowed for. The parables of commercial realism – the unjust steward, the talents, the two debts, the labourers in the vineyard – as well as the teaching about the danger of serving mammon and the confrontation with the wealthy young ruler all point in the direction of an economic radicalism of immense spiritual power. Those seeking the kingdom of God are to learn the opportunistic ways that belong naturally to those whose master is money. Translated into ecclesial realities in the earliest years of Christianity, the Epistles and Acts present us again with money as a crucial test of koinonia and discipleship. Ananias and Sapphira receive the wages of sin and the churches are galvanized into reflecting God's superabundant generosity in their response to the needs of the Jerusalem church.

It is crucial to be clear what this engagement with economic globalization on the one hand and Scripture on the other offers, and what it does not. There are no recipes here for deciding how to set interest rates or whether we should join the Euro, nothing to tell you how financial services should be regulated. Indeed, searching for such answers insulates one from the radicalizing possibilities in both directions, of engaging with Scripture and with the economy. On the other hand it does not allow the complacent assumption that as the Bible does not tell you how to run the world economy that means it effectively allows you to run it in its own way as long as you are decent and generous.[7]

This dialectical engagement constantly places alongside one another the global intentions of the Father of Jesus Christ and the operation of world markets, the latter constantly exposing with ever greater clarity the radical character of the former. Equally, the radical effects on the whole of our lives of the money-driven world economy are more and more exposed by engagement with Scripture. For as we spend more energy on anxiety about how to provide financially for our own futures, as we go on rewarding ever more substantially people whose lives are involved with moving money around, so our values, in every aspect of living, move further away from the globalizing ambition of God towards a situation where nearly every aspect of public policy and personal morality is fundamentally driven by globalizing mammon. My own testimony would have to be that if I were not committed to biblical engagement I would not have noticed these things, and as I notice these things so the radical demands of the gospel become clearer and clearer.

concluding observations

to be particular is not to be relative
To evaluate this case study, I return to the comment of Section 2 of *Lambeth 1998* that 'people are offered only opinions, not truth'. The causes of the relativism that flows from the globalization of the world economy are not far to seek, once the aims of that globalization are understood. Relativism is frankly more profitable. My engagement on behalf of the Church of England bishops with the affairs of the Church Commissioners is at the moment a huge area of learning. Recent correspondence between the Ethical Investment Advisory Group and a supermarket chain about Christmas Day opening reveals this point clearly: we only open because there are customers who want it; and as to staff objections, there is no need

to worry because there are now enough minority ethnic communities who are not Christian to staff the stores. It is clear that those comments are supposed to end the discussion: if people will pay for the goods and if there are people prepared to sell them for money, then that settles it.

But the prevalence of such relativism is no reason for abandoning our commitment to the particularity both of our situation and of the biblical witness. One of the most important sections of *The Interpretation of the Bible in the Church* comes in the introductory letter where the Pope links the task of biblical exegesis with the Incarnation, making the point that this is not to be limited to the earthly life of Jesus. The earthly life of Jesus is not defined only by the places and dates at the beginning of the first century in Judaea and Galilee, but also by his deep roots in the long history of a small nation of the ancient Near East, with its weaknesses and its greatness, with its men of God and its sinners, with its slow cultural evolution and its political misadventures, with its defeats and its victories, with its longing for peace and the kingdom of God.[8]

Where relativism takes the particular and limits its significance, an incarnational faith takes the particular seriously, whether it is the particularity of Scripture or the particularity of the global economy, precisely of its transcendent, universal significance.

the priority of the Gospels and the location of the Church's ministers

In the eucharistic liturgy the first Christological moment, the one that brings the assembly to its feet, is the reading of a passage from the Gospels.[9] Since Lambeth 1998 I have often asked myself what if anything was the cause, and what the effect, of our particular concentration on a Pauline epistle. There is every reason for taking the Pauline corpus seriously – that is not in question. But what the Gospels demand of us in particular is that we locate ourselves among the *disciples*, and that is our primary location. Locating ourselves with the apostle, with his trials and triumphs, and especially with the pressures on his leadership, played its part, I believe, in the pressure on us to resolve, to answer, to propose, to lead. Accordingly what the world heard was what we decided, and the pressure to decide is in my view related in some measure to what we were led to study and the particular way in which the bishops presented 2 Corinthians to themselves. If we are the guardians of anything it is of discipleship as the principal Christian mode of being before God, the one who calls us to encounter him through intense engagement with the Scriptures and the challenges of contemporary living.

uncertainty as the model for biblical obedience

The global market is an area of life where there is no difficulty obtaining agreement to the proposition that the Bible has no clear answers. The interesting thing is the power in our life as Church, of matters where it is assumed that the Scriptures do provide such clear answers. The disciplines we apply to the application of biblical understanding derive generally from those areas where we are inclined to believe that the Bible does provide clear guidance. Confronted with uncertainty we strive to get as near as we can to the certainty offered in other areas. Yet this excursion into the encounter between the Bible and the global economy suggests two things:

First, the all-consuming character of the globalized economy affects precisely those areas previously thought of as unalterable certainties. The so-called universal human experiences about which the Bible speaks are in fact radically particularized according to your place in the global economy, as creditor, debtor, rich or poor. Being born, eating, sleeping, making love, getting ill, dying – all these experiences are radically different according to where the globalized economy places you, and a morality that seeks to deal with those issues without taking that point into account will deal with them at an incredibly superficial level.

Second, focusing on a theme where we do not feel we have failed if we do not come up with definite answers opens up the encounter with Scripture as essentially an encounter with God and therefore with mystery. I hope I have indicated that the globalized economy offers itself to us as *mysterium tremendum et fascinans*, vastly exciting, overwhelming in its power and potentiality, an expansion of our horizons beyond our wildest imaginings, a real rival to the living God.[10] That being so, I cannot accept a doctrine of the word of God, or procedures with the Scriptures, that make them less exciting, less overwhelming in their power and potentiality, less ultimately mysterious, less radicalizing.

If one thing is beyond doubt in the globalization of the economy, it is that there is no way back to the mechanical world we have now left behind. We inhabit the global mystery of the market, and live before the unsearchable mystery of God into which the Scriptures invite us.

chapter 12

the World Faiths Development Dialogue

an interfaith response to poverty and development in an age of globalization

Wendy Tyndale

introduction

It was in February 1998, at Lambeth Palace, that the World Faiths Development Dialogue (WFDD) was born, out of surely one of the most remarkable gatherings that that medieval building has ever hosted[1]. Leaders from nine different religions from all over the world met for a day and a half to discuss the themes of poverty and development among themselves and with senior officials of the World Bank. The conference, chaired jointly by Dr George Carey, the Archbishop of Canterbury, and James D. Wolfensohn, President of the World Bank, revealed the different use of language and the different ways of thinking, as well as the different visions of the very aims of development, of the religious communities and the secular development agencies. Nevertheless, a spirit of enthusiasm was generated by a common commitment to justice and to a better deal for the poor, and it was decided to try to build bridges across the divide.

Since then the focus has been on conceptual work about the meaning of 'poverty' and 'development' and on what some of the fundamental criteria for development should be. No attempt has been made to reach a consensus among the faith communities, but WFDD's booklet *Poverty and Development: An Inter-faith Perspective* highlights much common ground that has been uncovered on many key issues.[2] It is on the basis of these shared principles that interfaith work has begun in Tanzania (on national health policies), in Ethiopia (on food security) and in Guatemala, where a group made up of Christians, Jews, Muslims and indigenous spiritual leaders is contributing to national thinking about the values underlying educational curricula.

No-one could pretend that such joint action by the faith communities is easy, and, as with any new venture, a dialogue with the powerful multilateral agencies involves risks on both sides. It may be necessary to take a few wrong routes before we discover the right one. But the potential of this unlikely partnership for bringing about real changes has so far kept us together, even if we may do quite a lot of arguing as we make our way along the road.

what can religious communities bring to such a dialogue?

practical engagement with the poor

Religious communities have networks among the poor and a depth of knowledge of the poor that are shared by few others. For thousands of years, faith-based organizations have been, in the best of cases, part of the poor. Many of their leaders are poor themselves, they live in poor areas and have poor friends. Moreover they do not tend to come and go. They stay where they are, firmly rooted.

Poverty is, however, only a 'virtue' if it is undertaken as a voluntary witness, and as a way of showing solidarity. There are no grounds in any religion for assuming that hunger and homelessness, for example, are the will of God or a manifestation of the divine order.

It is for this reason that religious organizations have always worked to counteract poverty, by charity originally, but increasingly in our times by providing services, such as health care and education, or programmes to open up economic outlets for peasant farmers, rural and urban artisans, fisherpeople and traders. They can give countless examples of ways in which, mostly at a local level, they have been successful in overcoming some of the most detrimental aspects of poverty. They thus have a key contribution to make to the improvement of the planning and implementation of development programmes (as well as a lot to learn from the planners and technicians of the official development agencies).

But even at this purely practical level, the faith organizations' strong sense of community and their vision of the ultimately transcendent reality of life mean that their aims go beyond economic improvement or the delivery of social services. Equally important to them are the generation of spiritual fulfilment and inner contentment and also human qualities such as hope and dignity.

Technical evaluators whose job it is to measure the impact of development work are hard pressed to include such unmeasurable elements in their assessments, but from the standpoint of the faith organizations, and the people with whom they work, these intangible results may, in the end, be more long-lasting, life-enriching and empowering than the quantifiable result of any project. How often have people said, 'My eyes were opened' or 'Now I feel brave', rather than mentioning the income they may have gained! Many of the debates within the WFDD arise from these considerations.

vision and values

In these critical times of globalization and rapid change, however, the faith communities are challenged to make a different sort of contribution, too, which reaches beyond their practical work. Today, as much as at any time in history, the world needs prophets who have the insights to understand what is going wrong, the courage to denounce it and the wisdom to make alternative proposals. Religious and spiritual leaders are called upon to be at the cutting edge of all key debates about the nature of the global society we are creating, or should create.

At the heart of this debate is the question of the aims and nature of the development process. Up to now this has been dominated by economists, who have focused on economic growth, rising income levels and technical progress. The challenge for the faith communities is to help to redress the balance by ensuring a vision beyond what is immediately tangible – by ensuring that the focus is on people.

A people-centred approach means that the aims of development will depend on an understanding of the very nature of the human being and will include the social, political, cultural, environmental and spiritual dimensions of life as well as the economic. Moreover, people will be in charge of their own development, so that the dreams of the Ethiopian man of abundant water and food for everyone and of 'neighbours who are happy and well', or of the Iranian woman who wants her village to become 'a place where my household and children [will] be happy and living among happy and prosperous neighbours', will be the aim.[3]

It is not a question of denying people access to the advantages brought by science and technology but of refusing to accept that the price for these must be the exclusion of the majority, the breaking up of social networks, the destruction of the environment and the loss of people's cultural identity.

It is a question of recognizing that the means by which development goals are reached are as important as the ends and that the desired ends will be different for different people from different geographical regions and cultural traditions. If growth and progress are about 'improvement', they must be about values, too, and thus about moral choices, which cannot be left to science to resolve.[4]

a different relationship between rich and poor

Globalization, in the sense of the integration of the people of the world into a single economic system, is not amoral or value-free. The stark contrast between the 'winners' and 'losers' whom it leaves in its wake has, up to now, meant that it is a very long way from reflecting the vision of the religious communities of a worldwide family based on relationships of compassion, trust and mutual respect.

It is not a case of evoking guilt among those who live in abundance, but of engendering a sense of responsibility towards those who can barely survive. It is a case of recognizing where there is a causal relationship between wealth and poverty and refusing to accept that the disparity between the rich and the poor is in any way unavoidable, 'natural' or justifiable.

There are many creative ways in which the rich can and do share responsibility with the poor, one of which is the Islamic system of lending money without interest, but allowing the lender to share any profits made. The multiple movements through which people in the North help to create fair trade networks with the South are another example, as are the credit unions and other forms of economies of solidarity created in poor communities in both North and South, often with initial capital from outside organizations.

Many of these initiatives are led or supported by religious groups. They should be more widely publicized as models that can be replicated and 'scaled up' so that they reach more people, but in the long run, the success of even these alternatives will depend on radical changes in international trade and financial and economic structures – on a balancing out of the unequal power relations between rich and poor.

a different relationship to the natural world

Just as societal relations cannot be value-free, neither can our relationship to nature. The utopia of 'development' providing limitless resources to meet unlimited needs is fast being exposed as a dangerous illusion, and pressure groups on all sides are pointing out the urgent need to exercise restraint and curb our destructive levels of consumption. There is even a growing understanding that to allow short-term financial profits to take precedence over life is to violate the cosmic order.

It is to this debate about restraint and the nature of the cosmic order that the spiritual and religious traditions have a great deal to contribute. Whether founded on the belief that the world belongs to the creator, or on a vision of human beings as an integral part of all creation, the teaching of all faith communities is that we have the responsibility to respect and take care not only of each other but also of the earth.

Religious institutions are still very large property owners in many countries of the world. Slowly but surely, from Bolivia to northern India, they are beginning to commit themselves to more ecologically sound management of the land in their possession, but their participation at the level of global debates on the environment could still be much more vigorous.[5] Such debates must include a focus on the difficult choices confronting us about biotechnology and genetic modification, about increasing food production at the cost of the long-term erosion of the soil and the daily destruction of scores of species. These are spiritual and moral choices, needing guidance of a kind that goes well beyond the competence of technical expertise alone.

challenges to the world's religious institutions

engagement with life around us

If the faith communities are to provide guidance to the contemporary world, they must be in a position to be able to act as catalysts for the generation of different insights into the burning issues of our day. The WFDD is an attempt to encourage people of different faiths to do this.

The challenge the WFDD faces is how to bring together in a meaningful debate people whose starting points are grounded in very different kinds of knowledge, on the one hand scientific analysis, based on proof, and on the other, an understanding that includes but transcends what is perceived – the kind of knowledge that has traditionally been known as wisdom. If the debate is restricted to what is pragmatically immediately useful to the practice of development experts, then the religious institutions will have nothing more to bring than secular agencies, but if the religious institutions are not able to clarify in practical terms what their beliefs mean for the aims and methods of development, their contribution will readily be dismissed as irrelevant philosophizing.

power

The WFDD has thrown up starkly the question of how spiritual and religious movements should engage with powerful worldly institutions. Attitudes to power are of particular concern in our day and age, when power is being accumulated in such a way that the decisions of a few corporations, and even individuals, can affect the lives of millions.

In their dialogue with the powerful of this world, it is the task of the leaders of the faith communities to give us practical insights into ways of exerting influence without entering into the worldly power game. Given the human nature of religious institutions, how can the WFDD prevent the subtle imposition of a different agenda of positioning for status, influence and money, an agenda that would soon render hollow any debate about sharing and caring for the dispossessed? Symbolic expressions of genuine concern can be the kinds of places chosen for conferences and meetings, as well as the ability to live generously but simply and to differentiate between respect and deference in the presence of powerful individuals and groups. But the faith communities will only manage to keep a distance from the seduction of power by holding on to the conviction, given to us by the wisdom of all religious traditions, that, because of their transitory and illusory nature, status, wealth and power are goals of little worth.

The question of power has also arisen, for the WFDD, within the religious institutions themselves. When, for instance, is it appropriate for well-known leaders to stand back and give space to practitioners who can speak from first-hand experience about work in poor communities? Another question is whether the WFDD can be led in such a way as to give expression to the movement as a whole, rather than to a few individuals at the top.

gender relationships

Although all religious traditions preach the virtue of equitable sharing, when it comes to the distribution of power among women and men, few positive examples come to the fore. Social inequity leads to material poverty, but it also leads to exclusion from full participation in cultural, political (and often spiritual) areas of life. The exclusion of women from education and opportunities to contribute equally with men in public life is having severe social and economic consequences for populations as a whole. It has been shown, for example, that the inequity in gender relations in Africa has been a major cause of low economic growth in many African countries.[6] It is also, with generalized poverty, one of the main reasons for the population explosion in our times, as well as for the spread of Aids.

In the light of the changing role of women in the context of globalization, the world's religions face the challenge of clarifying how much of the male domination habitual within their communities is based on their vision of the divine order and how much it stems from cultural traditions that could now be considered out of date. And they face the challenge, too, of defining what place women – who, with their children, are among the poorest people of the world – would have in a truly 'developed' society.

All gatherings and discussion fora of the WFDD, whether in person or by email, have up to now been largely made up of men, but a bird cannot fly with one wing only, as the Mayan people say. Unless a balance is sought, the world is likely to continue to flutter along lopsidedly, unable to take flight.

the need for joint action

In the twenty-first century's world of information technology and high-speed transport, sectarianism, often based on ignorance arising from a lack of communication, has no place. The WFDD is not advocating a merger of religious beliefs; on the contrary, the richness of diversity is one of the values it has been promoting most energetically. But amid the conflicts and destruction all around us, the religious institutions are called to lead the way, by demonstrating different modes of being which replace rivalry and adversarial behaviour by mutual respect, cooperation and solidarity. This is one of the main aims of the interfaith group in Guatemala, where rivalry and competition among different Christian groups as well as between them and people of other spiritual traditions has been a highly divisive force in that conflict-torn country.

engagement with secular development organizations

campaigning

Hitherto, if people from faith communities have engaged at all with the international financial institutions or multilateral development organizations, it has tended to be from the other side of the campaigning fence. A prime example of how religious communities campaigning together can make a difference was the Jubilee 2000 campaign for the cancellation of the unpayable debt of the most heavily indebted poor countries (HIPCs). Their message was that the international contracts concerning the payment of debts have led to morally unjustifiable injustice and suffering for millions of people in the world.

There is no doubt that this campaign contributed to changes in policy, both of the international financial institutions and of individual governments. The changes were achieved through the widespread raising of awareness, complemented by careful research and focused lobbying. Campaigning has thus proved itself to be an effective tool for change.

dialogue

There are many who fear that the strategy of dialogue involves too great a risk of being 'co-opted', or seduced by proximity to the powerful into adopting their agenda. But the WFDD has arisen out of the conviction that the widespread injustice, material poverty, violence and environmental destruction we see in the world around us call for the faith communities to look for new ways of bringing about changes in the situation. We are thus daring to say that the time has come for them to try to enter into a relationship of active dialogue and understanding with the international financial institutions and multilateral and bilateral government development agencies.

This does not mean that there is no longer any room for vigorous campaigning, nor does it mean a 'marriage' with the powers that be. But it is only through a serious conversation that people from the religious institutions will be able to respect the concerns of those who are trying to combat poverty from a technical and economic perspective. Only thus will they learn to understand the complexities facing the technicians. And, on the other hand, it is only through interaction with the faith communities that the secular world will ever manage to appreciate the validity of the faith communities' different way of understanding reality.

suggestions for action

Within such a relationship, the responsibility of the religions is to leave nothing to the 'experts' alone. The institutions of global capitalism may be able technically to function efficiently, but it is only if they work according to an explicit code of moral values that they will achieve socially acceptable results. Spiritual and religious leaders from both North and South, together with members of their communities, can contribute to practical efforts that are already under way, such as the establishment of codes of conduct for the multinational corporations.

At a national level, partly as a result of the Jubilee 2000 campaign, the governments of the most heavily indebted and poorest countries are now being asked by the funding agencies to engage with civil society and the private sector in drawing up Poverty Reduction Strategy Papers. These are to set targets and priorities for the use of available funds. With their intimate knowledge of the needs of the poorest communities and the moral authority they possess among the people, religious leaders are called upon to take part in these processes, to ensure that those in most need are the focus of attention. Collaboration with religious communities internationally may be a helpful way of lending more political weight to their participation and also of providing any information and technical help needed.

It is clear that faith-based development agencies such as Christian Aid, CAFOD or Muslim Aid have a key role to play in channelling resources to carefully chosen partner organizations and in providing technical expertise and information, but their legitimacy comes from the support they receive from their faith communities. It is the responsibility of the religious communities themselves to take action to raise awareness about issues such as the injustice of the current trading rules, or the evil and destructive nature of corruption – one of the main causes of poverty today.

Common to all the faith communities, however, is the belief that all these actions for social transformation will only be possible if individuals manage to undergo a change within themselves. Only by knowing ourselves more deeply can we reach a truer understanding of the world around us. Although there are, of course, plenty of religious people within the multilateral institutions, as institutions they are not likely to latch onto personal spiritual transformation as the key to combating poverty in the world. Nevertheless they are likely to be willing to work together with the religions in the broader area of personal transformation, which is the task of education – an area of work high on the agenda of the United Nations and the World Bank.

Maybe one of the major tasks facing religious – and humanist – organizations and individuals today is to point out that the International Development

Targets, set jointly by multilateral agencies and individual governments, cannot merely be about quantifiable statistics. They must also be concerned with the quality of the changes made. It is not just a question, for instance, of getting all children into school by the year 2015, but of educating them in such a way that they can make a contribution to a fairer and more peaceful society. A judge needs not only excellent knowledge of the law but also an understanding of compassion in order to mete out true justice. A politician will never truly represent the needs of the people unless he or she combines intellectual ability with a deeply rooted sense of integrity. Unless scientists have a sense of responsibility, they will end by causing havoc.

The WFDD is only one small initiative among many, whose aim is to bring more justice and peace to the world. The tasks it has set itself of achieving changes on both sides of the dialogue are formidable. On the one hand, by focusing on issues of common concern it hopes to generate greater solidarity among the different religious communities and also to encourage a critical appraisal of how their relationships, both with the powerful and with the powerless, might achieve more beneficial results for the latter. On the other hand, the aim is to raise more awareness within the multilateral development agencies of the need to look beyond the purely pragmatic and to place human beings right at the centre of development policies and practice. If the WFDD makes any contribution to these goals being met, its efforts will not have been in vain.

chapter 13
addressing exclusion in an urbanizing world

Andrew Davey

urban growth and division

During the first decade of the twenty-first century our world will reach the symbolic point when over half its population will live in towns and cities. Urban statistics point to the countries of the South as key to this urban revolution (see Figure 13.1). Cities with over 10 million people are becoming commonplace. Most cities with over 1 million inhabitants are to be found in Africa, Asia and Latin America; over a third of the population of these cities live below the poverty line. There are an estimated 100 million slum dwellers in the world's cities.

In Africa, only a third of urban households have running water, just one in ten have mains sewage.[1] The world is now an urban place. Cities are key sites in many of the strategies to eliminate global poverty and its impact.

Figure 13.1 UN projections of urban growth

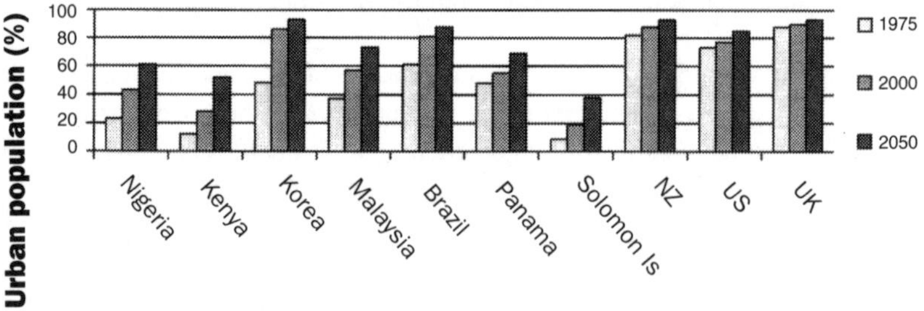

Source: *An Urbanizing World*, UN, 1996.

It is not just the speed at which our urban areas are growing that should concern us. The shape, the spatial dimensions, of the city are changing in ways we find hard to monitor or comprehend. The 'urban revolution' at the beginning of the twenty-first century goes hand in hand with an economic and technological revolution. One cannot speak about 'urbanization' without talking about 'globalization' – a process of change in technology and economics leading to greater and faster interaction between communities,

116

made possible through the ease of communications and travel. New forms of global culture and economic systems are emerging that transcend national boundaries and trading blocs – credit cards, banking, financial dealing, the Internet – all organized in and through cities: systems from which most of the world's poor are excluded.

the transnational city

Urbanologist Saskia Sassen describes cities as being strategic sites in a new geography of centrality and marginality that reproduces many of the old inequalities in new clusters, with no regard for national frontiers.[2] Globalization binds cities in new hierarchies according to the intensity of the transactions that pass between them. The most powerful of these are the international financial and business centres – including New York, London, Tokyo, Paris, Frankfurt, Zurich, Los Angeles, Sydney and Hong Kong.

A new level is emerging with cities such as Sao Paulo, Buenos Aires, Bombay, Bangkok, Taipei and Mexico City. On this second level, Sassen comments, 'there has been a sharpening inequality in the concentration of strategic resources and activities between each of these cities and others in the same country'. She goes on to observe: 'Alongside these new global and regional hierarchies of cities is a vast territory that has become increasingly peripheral, increasingly excluded from the major economic processes that fuel economic growth in the new global economy.'[3]

The cities of Africa do not feature in these hierarchies. Technological and economic apartheid is apparent in the continued exclusion of continental Africa from the connectivity that is emerging – what Castells has called 'the disinformation of Africa'.[4] Bishop Laurie Green has also commented:

we must take care not to be swept along with the rhetoric of globalisation studies to accept that the economically significant world cities are the only centres of power. For although economics is a tremendously powerful factor on the world stage there are other forces which are equally important for a Christian analysis.[5]

Sassen also detects that patterns similar to denationalizing processes associated with global capital are to be found in another key grouping in the contemporary city – the new urban poor, a mobile migrant labour force upon which the infrastructure of the global city depends. The claims that the poor, particularly women workers and migrant groups, make upon the city will become an increasingly significant part of the new transnational politics. This 'signals a politics of contestation embedded in specific places but transnational in character'.[6]

The global urban population changes with social transition, migration and community tensions. New demands are made on urban settlements to accommodate a vast array of groups and minorities within a common space. Competition and conflict, as well as new forms of cooperation and co-existence, accompany this process. In an age of globalization new forces are shaping settlements as new patterns of commerce and communication make many of the old foundations of settlements redundant. Employment becomes temporary and insecure; economic disparities become more apparent; migration makes many settlements transitional; the destiny of the urban area is determined by corporations and market forces that may be based on other continents. In some places high-tech towers rise in the core zones while new areas of residence, manufacture and leisure sprawl at the edges. In many other places impermanent settlements accommodate new arrivals, and city authorities are unwilling – or more often, in the face of readjustment programmes, unable – to accommodate or absorb those seeking a new life.

Those who do not dwell in urban areas are similarly affected through the dominance of the urban in a society's life: through urban-based media and national institutions, through the flow of goods from migrants, and through the ever-increasing demands made on agricultural production by the urban populace. Cities are changing, the urban experience is increasingly common. The impact of economic changes drives the poor to urban areas – to strug-gling cities as well as to highly developed centres where they fare little better.

towards an Anglican response

In the two years before the 1998 Lambeth Conference members of the Church of England's Urban Bishops' Panel became increasingly aware of the need to bring before the conference issues of urban mission and ministry in the new global context. The Anglican Communion is uniquely situated in being able to draw on the experiences of Christians in cities at different stages of urban growth and decline. Some parts of the Communion have been engaged for many years with a wide range of initiatives that have raised questions about mission and ministry priorities in urban areas. Other parts of the Communion are facing unprecedented challenges as the Church finds that its assets and plant are tied up in rural mission when there is a serious need to develop a pastoral infrastructure in new urban areas with appropriate training and resources for lay and ordained leadership.

In the Urban Bishops' Panel's discussions frustrations were expressed about the failure of the Communion to address the challenges posed by urbanization in a unified way. This lack of action exists despite the fact that urbanization figured significantly in the reports of the 1978 and 1988 conferences. The 1988 report stated:

> In the developing nations, it is rural poverty which drives people into the cities to search for jobs and survival. Around great cities like Mexico City, Sao Paulo, Rio de Janeiro, Lima, Ibadan, Nairobi, Johannesburg and Calcutta, vast shanty towns grow uncontrollably; barbed wire and security devices protect factories and gracious homes from the poor. Fear leads the better off to believe that the only answer lies in better law and order.

> There is a great challenge to national churches in such countries to avoid repeating the failures of European and North American Churches. Do they give to churches in poorer districts similar resources as to those in well-off suburbs where there are strong congregations? Do they believe God can plant strongly rooted churches within the most hurt parts of the cities, or do they expect only to recruit individuals whose ambition is to move out of such communities? Do they work for justice and better opportunities for the urban poor? These questions apply also in Europe, North America, Australia and New Zealand.[7]

The Urban Bishops' Panel was also able to draw on the experience of the Church of England in producing and putting into action the report of the Archbishop of Canterbury's Commission on Urban Priority Areas, *Faith in the City* (1985).[8]

A decade on from *Faith in the City* there was an awareness that the analysis needed to move on to understand better how global factors were playing a role in shaping urban communities and the congregations that witnessed and served in them. The panel was increasingly aware of the new analysis, including that of Saskia Sassen and how the global position of the Church must give it potential as a player in the new transnational politics. The deeply embedded transnationalism of the Anglican Communion gives it the potential to organize around significant concerns that are shared by the provinces, and the energy of its networks provides the capacity for this to happen.

During the 1998 Lambeth Conference work on the significance of the new urban context emerged in two of the four 'sections' into which the bishops were divided. In addition, two fringe events were organized – an evening presentation on the issues and concerns, and a weekend visit to east London where the stark contrasts of wealth and poverty, as well as the diversity of the global city, became quickly apparent to participants.

In the final week of the conference, thinking took shape in the section reports and resolutions. Section 2, following the theme 'Called to Live and Proclaim the Good News', reported:

> both urbanisation and globalisation are now out of control and are failing more and more human beings and human communities. They are in danger of destroying the very idea of the city, where all have a place, where the majority can find fulfilment, and where a society's cultural and spiritual achievements can be celebrated.

> Our concern for mission and evangelism has made us aware that whereas the most rapid growth of our church is in the rural areas of the developing world, the most urgent challenge of Christian belief and belonging is to be found in the cities. . . . The real challenge to Christian mission in the twenty-first century will be that of urban mission.[9]

Section 3, following the theme 'Called to be a Faithful Church in a Plural World', commented:

> The Church has an important role to play in helping individuals and communities come to terms with the global changes which urbanisation demands of them. . . . the Church is called to develop forms of evangelism and pastoral care which speak to our contemporary urbanised cultures. Laity and clergy need to be trained to analyse and engage these cultures from the viewpoint of their Christian faith and to challenge the exploitation and spirit of competition they espouse.[10]

In their final plenaries the bishops passed the following resolution:

This Conference:
a) calls upon the member Churches of the Anglican Communion to address the processes of urbanisation across the world, both in our cities and all other communities;

b) asks our Member Churches to give urgent attention to 'Living and Proclaiming the Good News' in our cities so that all that destroys our full humanity is being challenged, the socially excluded are being welcomed and the poor are hearing the Good News (Matthew 11.3); and in order to assist this priority in mission

c) resolves

i) to ask the Anglican Consultative Council [ACC] to give support to the formation of an Anglican Urban Network to share information and experience on urbanisation and urban mission;

ii) to support the establishment of a 'Faith in an Urban World' Commission, after due consultation with ecumenical bodies.[11]

Subsequent work has focused on developing proposals for the establishment of an International Anglican Urban Programme based on three areas of activity: a network, an action-research project and a commission.

an Anglican network

An official network needs to be formally 'owned' by the ACC and supported by the primates.[12] Approval for this was given by the joint ACC/Primates Standing Committee in October 2000. Each province will be asked to name their key players on urban issues who will then be invited to form the core of the network. This will be complemented by a wider mailing list of subscribers developed from the existing contacts. A subscription will be levied on mailing list members from North America and Europe.

Information exchange will be the primary task, with the development of a biannual newsletter. (The provision of material in several languages will be a key factor in enabling the network to be as inclusive as possible.) As clusters of network members emerge it may be possible to develop regional urban forums, which could feed into the Commission's consultations.

an action-research project

The following outcomes are envisaged during the initial action-research project in order to establish the programme and to lay a foundation for an urban commission:

● A directory of resources – listing theological, missiological and sociological resources for understanding the Church's mission in its urban context;

● Network administration;

- Publications: an established regular newsletter distributed to the network; a basic introduction and handbook on urban mission; a volume of stories of good practice; contextual/regional/thematic studies;
- A theological critique on projects relating to human settlements, such as the Habitat programme of the UNCHS and the World Bank's 'Cities without Slums';
- Accessible Internet resources;
- Regional consultations and reports.

It is hoped that the network will earth the project in the 'street level' experience of urban communities and congregations. Informal consultations have already taken place with Habitat and the UN Development Programme, non-governmental organizations and other groups working on these issues. It will be important to establish information sharing and collaborative action with such groups.

a commission

The initial phase of the programme will clarify the scope and composition of the proposed commission and make its recommendations in a report to the next ACC meeting. A commission is a mechanism through which a major piece of analysis and missiological work can be produced and addressed to the Anglican Communion. It should have an emphasis on listening to the experience of urban Christians and ministers, and the theology that emerges from their struggles, witness and practice.

Drawing on this and other relevant expertise, the task of the commission should be to report to the ACC and the next Lambeth Conference (if and when one is called) on Christian presence and witness in an urbanizing world from an Anglican perspective. This should include the challenges of urbanization and globalization, theological engagement, prospects for mission and resource sharing. The commission should make recommendations as to how training, resources and communications for urban mission, and its theological framework, might be developed on a sustainable basis within the Anglican Communion.

So far funding and capacity have been established for the initiation of an Anglican Urban Network. Initial discussion and fundraising are taking place for the other parts of the strategy.

It has become increasingly apparent that the work described above needs to relate to the reality of the Anglican presence in urban areas throughout the world. It needs to build on that authority to address the issues of globalization and urbanization, and other global initiatives addressing issues of poverty, community life and sustainable development in this rapidly changing context.

shaping the urban future

The UNCHS Habitat II conference in 1996 posed important questions about the future of urban settlements. The preparatory report, *An Urbanising World*, reflected on the positive and negative aspects of urban life, and on what makes a good urban settlement.[13] How might good governance combine with the concerns of the sustainability agenda? Subsequent programmes will be grouped around the three vital issues of urban governance, secure tenure and slums. The last of these will be developed with the World Bank as the 'Cities without Slums' programme. It is too early yet to offer an assessment of these programmes. The Habitat +5 special assembly in June 2001 will look at the broader progress of the Habitat vision. At the time of writing, the Anglican Urban Network is planning, as one of its first initiatives, to send a delegation as observers to that summit. The results of this summit as well as the impressions of the observers will then be shared through the network with the wider Anglican Communion.

The Urban Future 21 World Commission published a report in July 2000 that engages with many of these concerns. The report provides a glimpse of what a global commission might possibly deliver.[14] A collaborative project between the governments of Germany, Singapore, Brazil and South Africa offers analysis, prediction and the possibility of a different future, thus providing a key text in the preparation for the 2001 Habitat +5 summit. The commissioners divide cities into three types: the city coping with informal hyper growth; the city coping with dynamism; and the weakening mature city, coping with ageing.

Much of *Urban Future 21* is concerned with offering two scenarios – the current 'trend' or 'business as usual' scenario, and a 'bending the trend' scenario. Without significant intervention by governments and other interests the sustainability of the city will be threatened by overwhelming poverty, environmental problems or economic stagnation. These trends can be deflected if 'governments act, positively but sensitively to influence the driving forces'. Education, environmental controls, transport, governance, flexibility in housing, pensions and taxation are seen as key in the strategies that need to be developed.

The outlook is basically optimistic. Technology and capital accumulation will together bring millions of people out of poverty into relative affluence; technological progress and economic globalization will prove to be on balance benign forces; enlightened self-interest will win the day. This approach feeds the assumption that through competition cities develop and succeed, moving upwards through the three classifications.

There is much in *Urban Future 21* that cannot be ignored: the wealth of detail is staggering and the analysis is vital. But there is a need for others to develop analysis and research that bring players like the Urban Future 21 Commission into dialogue. The fate of our cities is too important to leave to a few government-funded initiatives, and far too important to leave to a laissez-faire global market The interests that lie behind certain aspects of urbanization and globalization need to be critiqued and exposed. New alliances need to be forged that include the poor as part of the solution and are not reluctant to use social justice as their driving force. Hopefully the network being developed within the Anglican Communion will begin to fill that vacuum and offer a kingdom vision of inclusion, engagement and renewal throughout our urban areas.

chapter 14

the role of British mission agencies and dioceses in international development

Mark Oxbrow

historical overview

For at least 150 years the Anglican mission societies were the most effective world development agents of the Church of England. Together they deployed large resources devoted to education, health and agricultural development in every continent outside Europe. Even today the school system in Uganda, agricultural colleges in India and community health programmes in Malaysia and Argentina bear the distinctive marks of their Anglo-Saxon missionary origins. In many cases the very concept of 'development', a product, it could be argued, of the European Enlightenment and Industrial Revolution, has been a missionary implant into cultures employing a very different human teleology.

In the aftermath of the two world wars the British Churches, deeply concerned for the plight of refugees in Europe and with issues of reconstruction and development in other parts of the world, took a new approach to development. Out of crisis response grew a new concern for aid and development, underpinned by a strong theological attachment to the concept of human dignity. At the same stage in history deep questions were being asked about the appropriateness of missionary activity and its painful associations with European colonization. It is not, therefore, surprising to find that, instead of further developing their commitment to development through the mission agencies, the Churches supported the establishment of new aid and development agencies. Mirroring the development of the Oxford Committee for Famine Relief (Oxfam), Christian Aid became the development arm of the Protestant Churches in Britain, closely followed by CAFOD and, at a later date, Tearfund, World Vision (UK), and others.

Large organizations do not change direction overnight. For many decades after the establishment of Christian Aid, the official aid and development arm of the Church of England, Anglican mission agencies continued their development work with partner Churches around the world. Their reluctance to hand over this work to Christian Aid, Tearfund, or another 'development' agency seems, however, to have stemmed from more than institutional inertia. There are at least three other factors that need to be considered and which have serious implications for future cooperation between mission and development agencies working with the Church of England. First, there are situations where development agencies, often because of their European governmental funding and cooperation with two-thirds world government agencies, are not able directly to assist specifically Christian development programmes. In these cases Churches will still, and regularly do, turn to the mission agencies for assistance. Second, there are those within the recipient Churches who would question the philosophy of development (with its focus on economic development) adopted by Western development agencies. They may prefer to work in partnership with agencies that are open to working with different models, perhaps those rooted in community transformation or personal sanctification. Third, there are serious questions asked within mission agencies, as well as by partner Church leaders, about the theological implications of a structural separation of mission and development within the ministry of any Church. We will return to these issues below.

Today most Church of England mission agencies continue to engage in a wide range of aid and development programmes with partner Churches around the world. The difference, however, is that now these programmes are more than likely to be run in partnership with one or more of the development agencies. In Sudan, for example, long-term personnel might well be provided by a mission agency, while the programme funding comes from Christian Aid and short-term personnel are provided through a link with a British diocese.

mission agencies and development

Within the Church of England the mission agencies have different degrees of commitment to development issues, partly because of the distinctive theological positions they hold but also, and perhaps more significantly, because of the nature of the partnership relationships in which they find themselves. In recent years these mission agencies have come together, under the umbrella of the Partnership for World Mission (PWM), and now work more closely with the Church of England Board for Mission, the Companion Diocesan Links and a number of overseas diocesan associa-tions.[1] Many of these agencies also work regularly in the ecumenical forums of the Churches Commission on Mission (CCOM)[2] and Global Connections.[3]

In all of these contexts they are able to critique their own, and others', engagement in development programmes. The larger agencies are also engaged in regular work and liaison with the International and Development Affairs Committee of the Board for Social Responsibility, the Anglican Communion Office, and the Secretariat at Lambeth Palace.

One important aspect of the life of the Church of England mission agencies is that while they remain agencies of the Anglican Church in Britain they are increasingly seen as agencies that operate internationally and ecumenically. Their policy on development, therefore, is just as likely to be shaped by consultation with African Anglican partners, or ecumenical partners in China and India, as by discussions within the Church of England. At least one of these agencies is actively investigating what it might mean to be internationally governed and directed.[4] As world mission increasingly becomes an activity of the South and of the materially poor, the question of the role of UK-based mission agencies will become more acute.

One other factor which must not be overlooked in any consideration of British Anglican involvement in development is that many individuals and Anglican parishes choose to engage with issues of international development not through Anglican agencies or Christian Aid but, instead, through interdenominational and non-denominational agencies. Agencies such as Tearfund, Samaritans Purse, Interserve and the World Development Movement have an increasing profile in Anglican parishes and find themselves listed in the Church of England Year Book.

the mission agency contribution to a cross-cultural theology of development

The incarnational nature of much mission agency work, and the high priority given by them to 'people-in-mission programmes', ensures that they continue to bring into the Church of England high-quality cross-cultural communication. In recent years the quality and quantity of this communication has improved as societies such as the United Society for the Propagation of the Gospel (USPG) and the Church Mission Society (CMS) have become agents for the movement of many categories of people from 'everywhere to everywhere'. British-born missionaries are increasingly becoming a minority group as 'study partners', 'interchange visitors', non-British 'mission partners' and young (and older) people on 'experience programmes' move around the world.

This new international fellowship of people in mission is beginning to challenge some of the theological presuppositions about mission and development in ways that the 'funding partnerships' more typical of aid and development agencies cannot. We now live in a world where the majority of Christians live in contexts of economic poverty and where the growth in mission activity emanates largely from the 'South'. Speaking out of such contexts, leading missiologists such as Samuel Escobar question whether economic development can ever be a primary Christian objective.[5] The juxtaposition of rampant materialism, or customerization, and declining religious adherence in the 'developed' North raises questions about the very nature of the development that might be appropriate for countries of the South. The Church of England mission agencies are well placed to bring this important debate into the Church.

mission agencies and community transformation

If economic development can no longer be considered a primary objective, are there other models with which Christians from the South and the North can work together? There are of course some religious traditions in which the concept of development itself would be questioned and in which the focus would instead be on attunement or harmony.[6] Christian theology, however, in all its major strands has always taught that there is an intended progression in human experience towards an as yet unattained fulfilment of the kingdom of God. Development then is an expected outcome of Christian believing. It is the nature of this development that is debated between different Christian traditions, and it is this debate that Anglican mission agencies, and bodies such as Christian Aware, make available to the Church of England.[7]

One alternative model, championed especially in Asia, is that of 'community transformation'. Exploiting to the full the paradigm of the kingdom of God, exponents of community transformation would suggest that the primary developmental objective of the Church should be the transformation of relationships within a community, in such a way that each person regains the ability to give full expression to the image of God in their lives, which is their birthright. A major aspect of this process of transformation will inevitably be the transformation of exploitative economic relationships, but this ceases to be the primary focus. Issues such as gender relationships, the reconciliation of the sinned against, the building of trust between different faith communities, and the honouring of the child and the elder all stand alongside the eradication of international debt and the balancing of international trade.

One encouraging feature of the Diocesan Companion Links has been the increasing number of Anglicans who are now visiting Christians in other parts of the world and there taking the opportunity to reflect on issues of development.[8] Christians Aware has been particularly active in this area, providing a wide range of opportunities overseas and in Britain for Church members to listen to representatives of Churches in the South and to explore with them what 'development' might mean both in their countries as well as here in Britain. Rather belatedly, the mission agencies are also now following in the steps of Tearfund and others in offering programmes of exchange and education for British Anglicans.[9]

evangelism and evangelization[10]

As alternative models of development are suggested by Churches in the South, and explored here in Britain, we begin to see a process of reintegrating 'mission' and 'development'. Mission agencies talk much more about 'holistic mission' and, drawing encouragement from the five marks of mission, return with confidence to the development agenda, while Christian Aid, under the leadership of its new Director, takes much more seriously its responsibility to act as the agent of Churches, which are by their very nature 'missionary'.[11]

In 1991 the South African missiologist David Bosch encouraged the world mission community to re-examine its missionary paradigms.[12] For many, whether they agreed with Bosch's propositions or not, this has been the beginning of a journey that has taken them beyond Matthew 28.19 to a new appreciation of the missionary imperative of John 10.10 (which of course is where our Orthodox colleagues have been since the tenth century!). If we can hold together the discipling of Matthew and the 'life in all its abundance' of John, then we might have both a new agenda for mission that is transformational *and* an agenda for development through evangelization.

The experience of many of us working in both mission and development agencies suggests that it is here in Britain that the mission/development divide is most keenly felt. It is in conversation with our partners in the South that we will find new ways forward in international development that are both profoundly Christian and at the same time effectively transformational.

transformation or development?

I have already suggested that development is a Christian concept and that part of the eschatological hope to which we bear witness is the developmental movement of individuals and societies towards the 'pattern of Christ' and the 'kingdom of heaven'. I would like to suggest, however, that biblical theology leads us to believe that we should look for more than development. The salvation story, biblically and historically, is one of development punctuated by more radical moments of transformation, the Incarnation and Resurrection of Jesus being obvious prime examples.

One of the major exponents of 'transformational development' in recent years has been Bryant Myers, the Vice-President for International Program Strategy at World Vision International. In *Walking with the Poor* he argues that poverty, economic poverty, is not an issue to be addressed directly but rather a symptom of a deeper 'dis-ease' and that we waste our effort if we seek to address only the symptom and not the cause. He sees the causes of poverty as relational. At one level this relational 'dis-ease' is inter-human and exhibited in deception, distortion and domination, but at a deeper level it is spiritual and finds its expression in identity crisis and existential angst. He maintains that:

> The good news is that through Jesus Christ there is a way out of sin towards transformation. The bad news is that if this news is not accepted there is a sense in which those who refuse sit wrapped in chains of self-imposed limitations. For the Christian development worker, there is an obvious implication. There can be no practice of transformational development that is Christian unless somewhere, in some form, people are hearing the good news of the Gospel and being given a chance to respond.[13]

Another author who comes at this whole question with a very different theological perspective is Walter Wink in his 'Powers' trilogy.[14] He too, however, refuses to engage with issues of development at a purely economic level but seeks rather to understand the spiritual powers, the 'principalities and powers' of biblical imagery, that are at work in the whole process of impoverishment and entrapment. It is only, he argues, through a spiritual engagement with these powers, empowered by the transforming Spirit of

Christ, that the roots of exploitation and poverty can be pulled up. Finally, reference should be made to the very significant work of Miroslav Volf who in *Exclusion and Embrace* has a powerful chapter on 'Oppression and Justice'.[15] The most powerful image adopted by Volf is of the Trinitarian embrace (the ontological unity of the Godhead) broken at the moment of crucifixion in order that humanity might be included in that same embrace and share an identity that is God's own.[16] When this is our transforming vision then community development, economic justice and the eradication of poverty are but stages on the journey.

advocacy

During the last five years, one of the most significant experiences for British Christians concerned about international development has been their participation in the Jubilee 2000 campaign for the eradication of unpayable debt. This campaign has also provided a useful example of how development and mission agencies can cooperate and each make a unique contribution. While the development agencies like Christian Aid, CAFOD and Tearfund were often able to provide the essential research data and macro-economic analysis, the mission agencies could provide effective links with Church and community leaders in the most indebted countries. A recent example of this was the way in which USPG and CMS were able to facilitate the coming together of a delegation of African church leaders to put their case at the meeting of the G8 countries in Japan at the start of the new millennium.

The Jubilee 2000 campaign is one example of the growing significance of effective advocacy work in a world in which rapid communication and globalization force us to reinterpret the meaning of 'neighbour' and even the biblical concept of the 'stranger in the land'. With their clear focus on incarnational mission and people-to-people programmes the Anglican mission agencies are well placed to facilitate advocacy work when it is requested.

If effective development begins, as I have argued, with the transformation of relationships then the role of the advocate can be highly significant. The advocate is the one who gives a voice to the voiceless and a face to the faceless. Much has been written post-Kosovo about the ethics of a war in which technology places such large physical and psychological distances between the combatant and the victim. The pilot flying in bright sunshine above the clouds sees nothing of blood and orphaned children; his preoccupation is with 'targets' and electronics. In similar ways the complexities of the market economy create distances between the Tesco customer choosing beans or cabbage and the children of the Kenyan farmer who grew the beans or the illegal agricultural worker in Lincolnshire who harvested the cabbage. In this situation it can be the diocesan development advisor or the representative of Christian Aid who gives a face and a voice to those who put food on our tables. The 'fair trade' campaign has, in a sense, been an advocacy campaign. Through the work of Christian Aid small boys in India, who would never themselves have found a voice with which to speak in those European homes adorned with the carpets they have woven, are seen and heard. The advocate in speaking truth creates a new relationship between the voiceless and the unhearing. I may still choose to buy the cheapest carpet I can find but the knowledge imparted by the advocate has changed the nature of the relationship. I now know that my comfort is at the cost of another young life and that knowledge has transformational potential for both the carpet weaver and me.

I have spoken of professional development workers as advocates, but in fact any Christian with a commitment to transformation and development can take up this challenge. Indeed many, in recent decades, have done just that by ensuring that Fair Trade products appear in their own supermarkets or that shopkeepers are made aware of the working conditions of those who manufacture the products they sell.

education for development

Issues of international development are often complex, and, as in most disciplines, practitioners develop their own language which can easily deskill members of our Churches who have a basic concern for development but are confused by the 'experts'. The mission agencies, development agencies and diocesan structures of the Church of England have a responsibility to facilitate an educational process that enables all Church members to engage with issues of international development in a way that is distinctively Christian. In the 1970s three books were published which grasped the public imagination and provoked considerable debate within the Churches. The first two were the two reports of the Club of Rome: the first, *The Limits of Growth*, unmasked the 'human predicament', while the second, Reshaping the International Order, published five years later, made proposals for global action. The most significant, however, was the third book, *North–South: A Programme for Survival*, published in 1980 and usually referred to as the Brandt Report.[17]

The list of publications, study courses and audio-visual resources emanating from Christian agencies in the wake of these publications is too long to reproduce here. However, it is worth noting that in the decade that followed the publication of the Brandt Report 'development education' was high on the agenda of many Churches. The Church of England's Board for Social Responsibility produced its own report, *Development Education for the Church of England*, which, significantly, began with a quotation from the Brandt Report.[18] The report ended with the intentionally empowering words from a former General Secretary of CMS, 'With the appearance of human reason, choice consciously takes over from chance the direction of the evolutionary process.'[19]

In comparison with the 1970s and early 1980s, the last 15 years have seen far fewer publications specifically aimed at development education within the Church. Reviewing the annual reports of Christian Aid over the same period one seems to detect a constant struggle to maintain a clear focus on development in a 'marketplace of charitable giving' that is far more interested in the quick fix of emergency aid and relief work. It seems that the concept of development is no longer a powerful motivator. Is this the result of a failure of the education process to which we committed ourselves in the 1980s? Or, does it belie a much deeper unease concerning the pursuit, or achievability, of international development as such?

the role of Companion Diocesan Links

Since the publication of the last major report by the Board for Social Responsibility on international development in 1986,[20] a major change within Church of England dioceses has been the development of the Companion Diocesan Links. If the way forward in development is to be found, at least in part, through the transformation of relationships between individuals and communities on a global scale, then these links hold much potential, especially when they focus on the exchange of personnel and experience rather than money. The links are very different in different dioceses but all of them have provided opportunities for learning through relating.[21] One aspect of these links that has yet to be fully exploited is the potential for using the professional skills of lay people within the dioceses, at both ends, in actions which foster transformational development.

Diocesan World Development Advisors

Within the Church of England there are 41 dioceses in which at least one person is designated as a World Development Advisor. Most of these appointments are part-time and some achieve a much higher profile within the diocese than others do. A wide range of job descriptions are in use but most of these focus on (a) the support of programmes such as One World Week, diocesan appeals, and Jubilee 2000, and (b) education in the parishes and the briefing of diocesan officials and committees. Most are also encouraged to network with other diocesan officers and the local representatives of development and mission agencies.

At the end of 2000 the Jubilee 2000 campaign was formally dismantled and One World Week announced that it was facing serious funding difficulties.[22] These two occurrences suggest that the time may be ripe for a redefinition of the role of Diocesan World Development Officers. Such a redefinition could release them from their role as 'development enthusiasts' within the dioceses and bring them centre stage as evangelists of a gospel that is quintessentially transformational of individuals, communities and international human society. In the proclamation of this gospel they will find strong allies in the Anglican mission agencies and Christian Aid, where a concern for the evangel of the coming kingdom is central.

chapter 15

Christian Aid and the Church of England

partners in development

Daleep Mukarji

introduction

Christian Aid is the largest Church-based development agency in the UK and Ireland. Its origins lie in the need felt by the British and Irish Churches to respond to the humanitarian crisis that unfolded in Europe after the Second World War. From 1949 to 1991, Christian Aid was a division of the former British Council of Churches (BCC). When the Roman Catholic Church joined the BCC in 1991, bringing with it its own development agencies (CAFOD and SCIAF), Christian Aid became a separate entity but remained in close relationship with the new instrument, Churches Together in Britain and Ireland (CTBI).

Christian Aid is now 'owned' by 40 'sponsoring Churches' representing most of the non-Roman Catholic denominations in the UK and Ireland. The Church of England has always played and continues to play a pivotal and active role in the work of Christian Aid in relation to its involvement and participation at board level and across British Christian Aid committees. The Church supports activities at the diocesan and parish level and a number of individual members who volunteer, campaign and support Christian Aid. On its behalf Christian Aid works directly and indirectly with the Anglican Communion in the 60 countries of the world where we currently give assistance.

Christian Aid undertakes a range of activities with the Church of England and its other sponsoring Churches. This includes all the work demanded by our 'flagship' annual event, Christian Aid Week, providing information to our supporters (especially at the parish level), working with young people, and establishing and deepening a range of links between people and parishes and our partners overseas.

Today Christian Aid is primarily a development agency, though increasingly it is drawn into undertaking emergency and rehabilitation work. Our development, humanitarian and emergency work is built upon three fundamental pillars which inform, influence and, at bottom, determine how we work, where we work, with whom we work, and for how long we work.

The first of these pillars is poverty and poverty eradication. Christian Aid exists not merely to help poor people by responding to need, but to have an impact, to work to eradicate poverty, especially the poverty of very poor people. In terms of how we work, we try to focus on where we can 'make a difference', building upon who we are, our own history, skills and experiences. Because poverty is manifested in different ways in different parts of the world we do not have a 'one size fits all' blueprint for 'doing' development. We examine each situation and work out how best we can use the resources we have to help the poor people we have identified as particularly needy.

This brings us to the second pillar of Christian Aid's approach to its work: the notion of partnership. With very rare exceptions, Christian Aid's development, advocacy and emergency work is undertaken with and through other organizations and agencies, which we term our 'partners'. Christian Aid is a non-operational agency. It is because we believe that eradicating poverty involves letting poor people take greater control of their lives that the thrust of our development work is built on the view that the best way to help is to assist and strengthen local individuals and groups.

The third pillar of Christian Aid's approach to development, advocacy and emergency work is the importance and influence our Christian roots have to and on our work. The term 'Christian roots' refers not merely to the (important) history of our links with our sponsoring Churches, but also to the thrust and orientation given to our current work. Thus we take seriously how the Christian faith can help us understand some of the issues of development, and we are inspired by a gospel that must mean good news to the poor.

In our recent vision statement, *Towards a New Earth* (March 2000), we affirmed our commitment to listen to, and to seek to inspire and serve, the Churches and individual Christians, 'enabling them to respond to the gospel as good news to the poor and put their faith into action'.[1] Thus we see Christian Aid as an integral part of the witness and service of the Churches in Britain and Ireland, linking them to the ecumenical family and our partners, working together to help people irrespective of caste, colour, creed or community. As a Church-related agency our essential purpose is to expose the scandal of poverty, to contribute to its eradication and to challenge the systems that work against the poor and the marginalized.

Christian Aid's campaigning work in the UK and Ireland

In recent years, a growing part of Christian Aid's work with Churches and church-based groups in the UK and Ireland has involved campaigning. We have put emphasis on our campaigning work for two linked reasons. First, we believe that eradicating poverty requires effective action and policy change not only at the local level but also at the international level. Second, we believe that policy changes can be decisively influenced by the often-prophetic activities of ordinary people, especially when they act together. We accept advocacy as an integral part of our mission.

In the last few years of the twentieth century our major campaign theme focused on unpayable Third World debt The Jubilee 2000 campaign gave the Church something to be proud of. At a time when the perceived wisdom was of the Church 'in crisis', fuelled by falling Sunday attendance, ageing congregations and a decreasing relevance to contemporary society, Jubilee 2000 showed the Church to be prophetic and effectively engaged in social justice issues. Although the campaign did not achieve the outright cancellation of all unpayable debts by the end of the year 2000, it was one of the most successful popular campaigns on development issues ever. Perhaps of greatest significance is that the IMF and the World Bank have been forced to acknowledge that poverty reduction should be part of their role, and new models of civil society involvement in monitoring debt cancellation have begun to emerge in highly indebted countries. This campaign has also been a very empowering experience for people who feel they can make a difference – they can influence the Government, the G8 and the international institutions.

Christian Aid's work with debt will continue as long as the problems persist. In the years ahead we will work with others – Churches, agencies and individuals – to ensure that the 'Jubilee movement' lobbies for debt cancellation with vision and strategy. However, the Jubilee 2000 campaign has to be seen in a wider context: debt cancellation would be worthless if it did not contribute to reducing poverty and to building a more just and healthy society. The Jubilee vision includes not only debt relief, but also taking care of the land, freeing the oppressed and enslaved and building a new community. It has always been about life, hope and a new start for the world's poor.

Christian Aid has often argued that although debt cancellation is an essential precondition for tackling poverty, it is not the only factor. Other economic issues are vitally important to poverty eradication, as are social issues such as participation, good governance and the strengthening of civil society. It is in this context that Christian Aid launched a campaign on trade rules at the beginning of 2001 which will be undertaken over the next four years.

Trade is fundamental to growth and development. Where debt has been a 'brake' on development, preventing poor countries from moving forward, a just global trading system has the potential to be the 'engine'. Global trade is huge and expanding rapidly: it now amounts to some £4 trillion each year, 15 times what it was at the end of the Second World War. Increasingly, the forces of the global market shape the terms on which people trade, how they produce what is traded, and what they are able to buy. Some poor people are excluded from trade altogether, while others are forced into trading relationships that are detrimental or, at the worst, exploitative.

Christian Aid's trade campaign, like the debt campaign, will be rooted in the Churches, including the Church of England. We will be campaigning for global trade rules to ensure that trade works in the interests of everyone, especially the poor and the excluded. We will also be working on the interaction between trade for the poor 'out there' and our own decisions as consumers and purchasers of traded products, not merely seeking to influence how we spend our money but looking closely at the activities of the companies who put the goods on our supermarket shelves and who purchase these goods from poor countries. This is all part of our wider effort to make a difference for the poor, complementing our work and activities within poor countries.

working with the Church ecumenically in poor countries
Since its establishment, Christian Aid has worked with the Churches in almost all of the 60 countries where it tries to give assistance. Because Christian Aid was founded and continues to be an expression of an ecumenical development and humanitarian effort, our Church relationships have tried and continue to try to reflect our ecumenical roots and continuing ecumenical make-up. Thus, our work with Anglican dioceses and parishes is related to our wider support for ecumenical development and emergency work overseas.

One indicator of our ecumenical approach and commitment is reflected in our funding profile. In the last financial year (1999–2000), Christian Aid channelled over £5 million to Christian development and humanitarian organizations. Given the ecumenical nature and roots of Christian Aid, we continue to channel substantial amounts of aid to the World Council of Churches and to a range of different councils of Churches. We are active in the ecumenical emergency alliance Action by the Churches Together (ACT) International, based in Geneva, which, as its name suggests, links together Churches and councils of Churches to provide a more effective mechanism for responding to emergencies.

However, our largest contribution to the development and humanitarian effort of the Churches is through our partnerships with different regional, national and local councils of Churches. It is through these fora in particular that our funds contribute to the development and humanitarian work of many different denominations affiliated to these councils. Councils of Churches in Africa continue to receive the bulk of these funds, accounting in the last financial year for over 80 per cent of all funds allocated to all councils of Churches. Outside Africa, many of our Church-based partners are both long-standing and important. These include, in Asia, our work with the Churches of North and South India, ecumenical development agencies in India, Bangladesh and China, and the Christian Conference of Asia. We relate to the Middle East Council of Churches, the Pacific Council and the Caribbean Council and also with national councils in Latin America.

Our ecumenical approach is also manifested in the work we undertake with like-minded northern ecumenical development agencies. In particular, we join with other, especially European, Church-based organizations to provide a combined (and thus we hope more effective) use of Church funds and talents from a range of countries. We are linked formally within the Association of World Council of Churches Related Development Organizations in Europe (APRODEV) and with our sister organizations in North America, Australia and New Zealand.

In many countries where we work, programme officers from these organizations meet regularly to share and pool information on country situations and contexts. We recently began a process of trying to work even more closely together in five countries, with Christian Aid leading the process in the case of Malawi. We have also been involved in drawing up a joint ecumenical approach to our work in Israel/Palestine, which will provide the framework for the development and advocacy work of many of us over the next few years.

working with the Anglican Communion

Besides working with the Anglican Communion indirectly through the wider ecumenical movement, Christian Aid continues to work directly with the Anglican Church in a range of emergency and development projects in many parts of the world. We work predominantly with the Anglican Communion in Africa, South Asia and the Caribbean. It is to be noted that our European partners also support the Anglican Communion directly or indirectly in a variety of situations.

Christian Aid continues to support a range of different activities, moving away, over time, from a dominant focus on direct development projects for particular groups of poor people to embrace, as well, programmes focused on income generation, peace building, support for women and other marginalized groups, capacity building initiatives, monitoring the delivery of government services and, most recently, work linked to advocacy and building democratic structures and processes. However, activities in the areas of agriculture, food security, land development and reclamation, health and education still feature prominently in the work of the Anglican Communion supported by Christian Aid.

Most of Christian Aid's Anglican partners are long-standing and have been funded for many years. One recent trend in Asia has been a move away from the funding of individual dioceses to more core support for the Church of North India at the synodical level. This initiative was taken not only by Christian Aid, but also with sister Church agencies in Germany and the Netherlands. The aim is to help build the overall capacity of the Church, including clergy and other church leaders, focusing especially on projects to address the needs of poor Dalits, women and Adivasis. In Asia, Christian Aid continues to give significant support to the Church of South India, especially to its Board of Diaconical Ministry, while in Bangladesh, the Church of Bangladesh remains a long-standing partner.

A few examples from Africa provide something of the content and 'flavour' of the development work of the Anglican Church that is supported by Christian Aid. It has long supported the work of the Anglican Church of Tanzania. At the national level it is helping to fund a central programme of training for diocesan staff involved in development projects, while continuing to fund some of the work of individual dioceses. Thus, the Diocese of South West Tanganyika's community-based health care and safe water projects are supported by Christian Aid, as well as by the Leicester Diocese and the

Church of Ireland. The Diocese of Central Tanganyika's food security programme is currently supported by Christian Aid, involving not only support for agriculture and the development of shallow wells but also leadership training. The Diocese of Ruvuma's agricultural projects are supported by Christian Aid, while the Diocese of Mpwapwa's programme to address environmental degradation also benefits from a Christian Aid grant, as does a loan fund to help villagers purchase seeds and tools for planting. More recently, Christian Aid has funded food distribution initiatives both in the Mpwapwa Diocese and in the Dioceses of Zanzibar and Tanga.

In Kenya, Christian Aid funds centrally the work of the Anglican Church of Kenya, as well as some local initiatives such as the work of the Ukamba Christian Community and the Pwani Christian Community Services for Community Development work, the latter being an agriculture and health project covering 21 villages in Kilifi District. A grant has also been given to help develop and deepen institutional development initiatives with multiple stakeholders across the Church. In Sudan, direct grants have been given over the past year to the Dioceses of Bor, Cuibet and Mundri, Rokon and Lainya, Yambio and Lui. These grants have supported work in the fields of peace and reconciliation initiatives, education and schooling, food security and vocational training. Various grants have also been given to the Episcopal Church of Sudan. In southern Sudan, in particular, Christian Aid has funded new efforts at peace building and initiatives aimed at strengthening civil society.

In Malawi, work on adult literacy, agriculture and water is currently being funded by Christian Aid. In the Livingstonia Synod the water project is targeting over 50,000 beneficiaries. The Blantyre Synod programme 'Development Through Literacy', which is concentrated on 45 literacy centres in the south of the country, many located in church buildings, is the focus of the Ireland Millennium Appeal for Malawi through Christian Aid. In Uganda, support to the Church of Uganda and a number of dioceses (including Sorioti and Busoga) has focused on support to the Church's Planning, Development and Rehabilitation Department and on agricultural and food security programmes.

Christian Aid has also been able to assist Church leaders, including Anglican bishops and key development workers, in undertaking a range of development and humanitarian initiatives, as well as to assist their advocacy work through support from our advocacy, media and campaign teams.

We also have the opportunity of enabling and supporting some key Church leaders in their own training and development.

the future

What will be the future of our relationship with our ecumenical and denominational partners in our development and emergency work? Our work will continue to be informed and profoundly influenced by the three 'pillars' mentioned above: the focus on poverty, the importance of partnerships and our Christian roots.

In the near term, we are planning for a steady expansion of our international work, especially our development and advocacy work, made possible by an anticipated increase in our core income. We have committed ourselves, in the words of our *Corporate Plan*, 'to continue to deepen and expand the quality of our relationships with our core partners which will necessitate a continual review to reduce the number of partners with whom we work'.[2] This does not mean that we rule out developing new partnerships in the future, but it does indicate that we will review the thrust and nature of our projects and programmes and the quality of our partnerships. This means that we will not be encouraging a massive increase in new programmes with new partners. Christian Aid simply does not have the human resource capacity to receive and process applications for assistance from a number of new potential partners. We need to say 'no' just to maintain the quality and impact of our current programmes.

Within this overall context, the following checklist shows the issues Christian Aid currently sees as important in developing and furthering current programmes in the countries in which we operate:

- We wish to continue, indeed to deepen, our commitment to supporting the development and emergency work of the ecumenical family. It is in this context that we will continue to stand ready to work with denominational partners.
- We wish to support partners in terms of their abilities and capacities to respond to disasters and emergencies.
- We will continue to support partners in terms of helping them to strengthen their organizations and build their own capacities to undertake development work.
- We will support partners in helping them to empower the poor and enhance the development impact on the poor of the work they undertake

by sharing with them our own skills and insights in relation to capacity building, appraisal monitoring and evaluation and through helping them network with other relevant organizations.

- We will support partners in their work in the area of advocacy, helping them to increase and enhance their own voice and influence, both individually and as members of civil society, thereby improving the chances and opportunities of the poor whom they serve.
- We will continue to respond to need by assessing requests from partners to support discrete projects and programmes that aim to meet the immediate needs of particular groups of poor people.

conclusion

As an agency of the Churches in Britain and Ireland, Christian Aid seeks to be flexible, supportive and innovative in its partnerships with the Churches here as they consider new ways to pray, act and give. We want to work with different parts of the Church of England, at a variety of levels in relation to development, to see how together and on its behalf we can make a difference in places where we work through local partners. We are proud of this long-standing partnership with the Church of England. We recognize the need to continue to nurture this partnership so that together we can build up a movement for justice with people committed to campaigning for change – to build a new global society in the perspective of the reign of God. As Christians, we say 'we believe in life before death'. We want this fullness of life to become a possibility for all people, especially the poor and the marginalized.

Our Government and the international community have made a commitment to halving the proportion of people who live in absolute poverty by 2015 by taking 1 billion people out of poverty. They are also committed to universal primary education, basic health care and sustainable development. The Churches have a role to play in this. We need to hold our world leaders accountable to these international development targets. Together we have had an impact in the past. The challenge ahead is to work with others in building a new earth – where peace, justice and inclusion are a reality.

notes

chapter 1: globalization and the Church: an overview

1. Samuel Huntington, *The Clash of Civilizations and the Remaking of the World Order*, Simon and Schuster, New York, 1996.

2. John Gray, *False Dawn: The Delusion of Capitalism*, Granta, London, 1998, p. 3.

3. Peter Selby, *Grace and Mortgage*, Darton, Longman and Todd, London, 1998.

4. Quoted in Chris Patten, *Globalisation and the Poor*, Cardinal Hume Memorial Lecture, St Mary's Cathedral, Newcastle upon Tyne (available from Cathedral).

5. Albert Nolan, *God in South Africa*, CIIR, London, 1998, p. 10.

6. World Bank, *2000 World Development Report*, Washington, D.C., summary paragraph 13. For a more extended treatment of this theme see David Green and Catherine Melamed, *A Human Development Approach to Globalisation*, June 2000, Christian Aid and CAFOD paper submitted to DfID, London.

chapter 2: the role of the Church in overseas development

1. Michael Taylor, *Not Angels but Agencies: The Ecumenical Response to Poverty – A Primer*, SCM/WCC Risk series, 1995, p. 30.

2. For the significance of Olaudah and Wheatley see Paul Gilroy, *Between Camps: Race, Identity and Nationalism at the End of the Colonial Line*, Allen Lane, London, 2000.

3. A detailed exposition of this theme is contained in the two volumes of Jean and John Comaroff (eds), *Of Revelation and Revolution*, Chicago, 1991 and 1997.

4. See Lamin Sanneh, *Encountering the West: Christianity and the Global Cultural Process: The African Dimension*, Marshall Pickering, London, 1993.

5. See, for example, Susan Billington Harper, *In the Shadow of the Mahatma: Bishop V.S. Azariah and the Travails of Christianity in British India*, Curzon Press, London, 2000.

6. David Goodhew, 'Working-class respectability: the example of the western areas of Johannesburg, 1930–55', in *Journal of African History*, vol. 41, 2000, pp. 241–66.

7. David Maxwell, 'Delivered from the spirit of poverty?: Pentecostalism, prosperity and modernity in Zimbabwe', *Journal of Religion in Africa*, vol. 28, 1998, pp. 350–73.

8. Bernice Martin, 'From pre- to postmodernity in Latin America', in Paul Heelas (ed.), *Religion, Modernity and Postmodernity*, Blackwell, Oxford, 1998, pp. 102–46.

9. The World Lutheran Federation has been the exception, but since the unification of Germany, the amount of resources available from the German Protestant Churches has declined.

10. The Uganda Christian University exists on the campus of the Bishop Tucker Theological College at Mukono. The theological college is part of this larger institution. The author was a teacher in this college from 1976 to 1990 and is ordained in the Church of Uganda.

11. Aili Mari Tripp, *Women and Politics in Uganda*, James Currey, Oxford, 2000.

12. John Waliggo, 'A woman confronts social stigma in Uganda', in J. F. Keenan, SJ (ed.), *Catholic Ethicists on HIV/AIDS Prevention*, London, 2000.

13. Paul Gifford, *African Christianity: Its Public Role*, Hurst, London, 1998, especially sections on 'neo-patrimonialism' and 'externality'.

14. 'Eating' is a euphemism for corruption.

15. Pervaiz Sultan, 'The involvement of the Church of Pakistan in development', PhD diss., Open University, 1997.

16. Timothy Longman, *'Commanded by the Devil': Christianity and Genocide in Rwanda.* Manuscript under consideration for publication.

17. Desmond Tutu's introduction to Paul Germond and Steve de Gruchy (eds), *Aliens in the Household of God: Homosexuality and Christian Faith in South Africa*, David Philip, Cape Town, 1997.

18. Charles Villa-Vicencio and Wilhelm Verwoerd (eds), *Looking Back, Reaching Forward: Reflections on the Truth and Reconciliation Commission of South Africa*, Zed Books, London, 2000.

19. Stephen Ellis, *The Mask of Anarchy: The Destruction of Liberia and the Religious Dimension of an African Civil War*, London, 1999.

20. Heike Behrend, *Alice Lakwena and the Holy Spirits: War in Northern Uganda, 1986–97*, James Currey, Oxford, 1999.

21. I intend to write further on this subject. An account can be found in the Annual Newsletter of the Uganda Church Association for 1999 (ed. Kevin Ward, printed in Halifax).

22. See Marc Nikkel, 'Children of our fathers' divinities or children of Red foreigners?', in Andrew Wheeler (ed.), *Land of Promise: Church Growth in a Sudan at War*, Paulines Publications, Nairobi, 1997. The book is part of the impressive 'Faith in Sudan' series which Andrew Wheeler and other Sudanese experts have been working on for a number of years. Marc, priest and missionary of the Episcopal Church of the United States and of the Church Mission Society, worked tirelessly for the Church and for peace in Sudan until his death from cancer on 2 September 2000.

23. Celestin Monga, *The Anthropology of Anger: Civil Society and Democracy in Africa*, Lynne Riener, London, 1996.

24. Celestin Monga, *The Anthropology of Anger*, p. 114.

chapter 3: General Synod and international development

1. General Synod, February Group of Sessions 1975, *Report of Proceedings*, Vol. 6, No. 1, p. 20.

2. General Synod, July Group of Sessions 1981, *Report of Proceedings*, Vol. 12, No. 2, p. 550.

3. General Synod, *The Brandt Commission Report: A Report by the Board for Social Responsibility*, Church House Publishing, London, 1980, p. 5.

4. General Synod, February Group of Sessions 1972, *Report of Proceedings*, Vol. 3, No. 4, p. 769.

5. General Synod, *Let Justice Flow: A Report by the Board for Social Responsibility*, Church House Publishing, London, 1986.

6. The main workers in development education within the Church are the Diocesan World Development Officers who are appointed by their dioceses and are responsible in general either to a Board for Social Responsibility or to a Board for Mission and Unity. These development workers are generally unpaid and reflect the voluntary spirit that often underpins so much of the Church's work.

7. General Synod, February Group of Sessions 1972, *Report of Proceedings*, Vol. 26, No. 2, p. 723.

8. Anne Pettifor, *The World Will Never Be the Same Again: Introduction to the Jubilee 2000 Coalition Final Report*, 2 December 2000, p. 2.

9. General Synod, *Faith in a Global Economy: A Report by the Board for Social Responsibility*, Church House Publishing, London, 1998.

10. General Synod, *Faith in a Global Economy*, p. 22.

11. General Synod, *Responsibility in Arms Transfer Policy: A Report by the Board for Social Responsibility*, Church House Publishing, London, 1994, p. 6.

12. These countries include Burundi, Central African Republic, Congo, Democratic Republic of Congo, Ethiopia, Liberia, Myanmar, Sierra Leone, Somalia and Sudan.

13. General Synod, *Responsibility in Arms Transfer Policy: A Report by the Board for Social Responsibility*, Church House Publishing, London, 1994.

14. General Synod, *Responsibility in Arms Transfer Policy*, pp. 46–7.

15. House of Commons, International Development Committee, Sixth Report, *Conflict Prevention and Post-Conflict Reconstruction*, Vol. 1, 1999, p. 5.

16. I am grateful to Mr Neville White of CCLA Investment Management Limited for advice and guidance on the work of the Ethical Investment Working Group as well as the nature of investments made by relevant Church bodies.

17. Interagency Group on Breast-feeding Monitoring, *Cracking the Code: Monitoring the International Code of Marketing of Breast-milk Substitutes*, London, 1997.

18. General Synod, *Promotion of Breast Milk Substitutes: A Report by the Board for Social Responsibility*, Church House Publishing, London, 1997, p. 1.

19. Anna Taylor, 'Violations of the International Code of Marketing of Breast Milk Substitutes: prevalence in four countries', *British Medical Journal*, vol. 316, April 1998, pp. 1117–22.

20. General Synod, February Group of Sessions 1998, *Report of Proceedings*, Vol. 29, No. 3, p. 880.

21. General Synod, July Group of Sessions 1981, *Report of Proceedings*, Vol. 12, No. 2, p. 515.

22. The World Bank, *World Development Report 2000/2001: Attacking Poverty*, OUP, Oxford, 2000, p. 3.

chapter 4: the UK's aid programme

1. This chapter draws on various reports by the Department for International Development, the Foreign and Commonwealth Office, the World Bank and the World Trade Organization. Readers might find several of the House of Commons International Development Committee's reports (1997–2000) of interest. A number of Christian Aid research reports are also of value when considering the effectiveness of the UK's aid programme.

2. White Paper on International Development, *Eliminating World Poverty: Making Globalisation Work for the Poor*, December 2000.

3. DTI, *Review of ECGD's Mission and Status*, 25 July 2000.

chapter 5: HIV/Aids

1. Peter Piot, Executive Director UNAIDS, as quoted in *Report on the Global HIV/AIDS Epidemic*, UNAIDS, Geneva, June 2000.

2. Kassinga is not the area's real name.

3. An orphan is defined as a child who has lost mother or both parents before the age of 15.

4. All figures taken from the *Report on the Global HIV/AIDS Epidemic*, UNAIDS, Geneva, June 2000.

5. Anne Skelmerud and Christopher Tusubira (eds), *Confronting AIDS Together: Participatory Methods of Addressing HIV/AIDS*, DIS, Oslo, and WCC, Geneva, 1997.

6. Noerine Kaleeba, Joyce Namulondo Kadowe, Daniel Kalinaki and Glen Williams (eds), *An Open Secret*, published by ActionAid, July 2000. Available from TALC at PO Box 49, St Albans, Herts, AL1 5TX.

7. For example, the Anglican Churches in Uganda and South Africa, the Roman Catholic Churches in Tanzania, Burundi and the Democratic Republic of Congo, the Salvation Army in Zambia and Kenya, the Presbyterian Church of East Africa.

8. *Report on the Global HIV/AIDS Epidemic*, UNAIDS, Geneva, June 2000.

chapter 6: the environment

1. General Synod, *Let Justice Flow: A Report by the Board for Social Responsibility*, Church House Publishing, London, 1986, p. 3.

2. General Synod, *Let Justice Flow*, p. 32.

3. David Gosling, *A New Earth*, CCBI/Delta Press, London, 1992, pp. 62–4.

4. David Gosling, *A New Earth*, pp. 103–4.

5. *The Economist*, 23 September 2000, p. 97.

6. General Synod, *Let Justice Flow*, p. 15.

7. Fred Pearce, 'That sinking feeling', *New Scientist*, 23 October 1999, pp. 20–21; Mike Hulme, 'Choice is all', *New Scientist*, 4 November 2000, pp. 56–7.

8. Jean Drèze and Amartya Sen (eds), *India: Economic Development and Social Opportunity*, Oxford University Press, Oxford, 1996, p. 10.

9. David Gosling, *A New Earth*, p. 14.

10. David Gosling, *Religion and Ecology in India and Southeast Asia*, Routledge, London, 2001, p. 154.

11. Michael Amaladoss (ed.), *Globalisation and Its Victims*, ISPCK, London, 1999.

12. David Gosling, *A New Earth*, p. 2.

13. For further information contact Claire Foster, Board for Social Responsibility of the Church of England, or David Pickering, *Going for Green*, Elizabeth House, Wigan WN3 4EX.

chapter 7: the role of business in development

1. *Effects of UK Investment Overseas*, Final (15) 1968 and Interim (12) 1967 Reports, Cambridge University Press.

2. Clare Short has made her observations about investment in East Asia and the resulting reduction of poverty fairly consistently in a number of speeches.

3. MIGA is the World Bank's Multilateral Investment Guarantee Agency (and with the IBRD itself, the IFC, the IDA and the ICSID, forms the Bank's family of institutions). It was established in 1988 (incidentally with the strong support of the CBI and its large members working with the

FCO's Overseas Development Administration – DfID's predecessor). Its main objective is to encourage the flow of foreign direct investment to developing countries by providing investment guarantees against non-commercial risks, e.g. currency transfer, expropriation or war. Though technically a separate entity from the World Bank, it draws on and shares certain Bank services.

chapter 8: corruption

1. This chapter draws on various reports by the Department for International Development, the Foreign and Commonwealth Office, the World Bank and the World Trade Organization. In addition, readers might like to refer to a number of articles on corruption and the need for good governance which have been produced by the Centre for Accountability and Debt Relief.

chapter 9: trade

1. Jagdish Bhagwati, *Free Trade, Fairness and the New Protectionism*, IEA Occasional Paper 96, 1995.

2. *The Challenges of a New Round of International Trade Negotiations – Trade for Development?* Oxfam-Solidarity, Belgium, 1999; *Understanding Global Issues: Fairer Global Trade? The Challenge for the WTO*, Understanding Global Issues Limited, London, 1996.

3. White Paper on International Development, *Eliminating World Poverty: Making Globalisation Work for the Poor*, December 2000.

4. Gerald Karl Helleiner, *Markets, Politics and Globalisation: Can the Global Economy be Civilised?*, UNCTAD, 10th Raul Prebisch Lecture, December 2000.

chapter 10: global institutions

1. Ngaire Woods, 'The challenge to international institutions', in Ngaire Woods (ed.), *The Political Economy of Globalisation*, Macmillan, London, 2000.

2. Duncan Green, *Capital Punishment*, CAFOD, 1998.

3. Statement released in Seattle, 2 December 1999.

4. For more details see *Forever in Your Debt*, Christian Aid, 1998.

5. For more details see *A Human Development Approach to Globalisation*, Christian Aid/CAFOD, 2000.

chapter 11: the silent word still speaks

1. This chapter is a revised version of a paper given at a meeting of the Bishops of the Church of England, the Church of Ireland, the Episcopal Church of Scotland and the Church in Wales in June 2000, devoted to the interpretation of Scripture.

2. *Official Report of the Lambeth Conference 1998*, Morehouse, London, 1999, p. 120.

3. Francis Watson, *Text, Church and World*, T. & T. Clark, London, 1994, p. 152.

4. Luke 12.2.

5. John Goldingay, *Models for Scripture*, Eerdmans, Carlisle, 1994.

6. See David Jenkins, *Market Whys and Human Wherefores*, Cassell, London, 1999; Michael Rowbotham, *The Death Grip*, Jon Carpenter, London, 1998, and *Goodbye America!*, Jon Carpenter, London, 2000; Rob van Drimmelen, *Faith in a Global Economy*, WCC, Geneva, 1998; George J. Benston, *Regulating Financial Markets*, IEA, 1998.

7. I find it difficult to describe Stephen Green's *Serving God, Serving Mammon?*, Marshall Pickering, London, 1996, in any other way, much as I respect the fact that it is based on very detailed and successful involvement in the financial markets.
8. The Pontifical Biblical Commission, *The Interpretation of the Bible in the Church*, Editions Paulines, 1994, p. 13.
9. The Pontifical Biblical Commission, *The Interpretation of the Bible in the Church*, p. 120.
10. I find Anthony Thiselton's use of the metaphor of 'horizons' particularly fertile. See his *The Two Horizons*, Paternoster, London, 1980.

chapter 12: the World Faiths Development Dialogue

1. Special thanks for their support and advice to the sisters of the Convent of the Incarnation, Fairacres, Oxford.
2. World Faiths Development Dialogue, *Poverty and Development: An Inter-faith Perspective*, Oxford, 1999.
3. Majid Rahnema, 'A development worker's second thought', *Compass*, Toronto, November/December 1995.
4. Chowdhry Kamla, *The Meaning of Progress*, 20th Anniversary Lecture, Institute of Rural Management, Anand (IRMA), December 1999.
5. See initiative with the Alliance of Religion and Conservation: http://panda.org/livingplanet/kathmandu.cfm.
6. *Gender, Growth and Poverty Reduction in Sub-Saharan Africa*, World Bank Special Program of Assistance for Africa, 1998.

chapter 13: addressing exclusion in an urbanizing world

1. David Sattherwaite, 'Will most people live in cities?', *British Medical Journal*, vol. 321, November 2000; Department for International Development, *Developments – The International Development Magazine*, Issue 10, 2000. See also the DfID's web site at http://www.developments.org.uk.
2. Saskia Sassen, 'The global city: strategic site/new frontier', in Engin F. Isin (ed.), *Democracy, Citizenship and the Global City*, Routledge, London, 2000.
3. Saskia Sassen, 'The global city', p. 51.
4. Manuel Castells, *End of Millennium*, Blackwell, London, 2000, p. 95.
5. Laurie Green, *The Impact of the Global: An Urban Theology*, Urban Theology Unit/UBP, p. 16. The second edition of this publication is due in 2001.
6. Saskia Sassen, *Globalisation and its Discontents*, New Press, New York, 1998, p. xxxiv.
7. Official report of the Lambeth Conference 1988, Morehouse, London, 1989.
8. Archbishop of Canterbury's Commission on Urban Priority Areas, *Faith in the City*, Church House Publishing, London, 1985.
9. Official Report of the Lambeth Conference 1999, Morehouse, London, 1999, p. 67.
10. Official Report of the Lambeth Conference 1999, Morehouse, London, 1999, p. 88.
11. Official Report of the Lambeth Conference 1999, Morehouse, London, 1999, p. 152.
12. The Anglican Urban Network described in this article is in the process of formation. All

inquiries should be addressed to The Revd Dr Andrew Davey, Board for Social Responsibility, Church House, Great Smith Street, London SW1P 3NZ. Email: andrew.davey@c-of-e.org.uk

13. See the Habitat web site at http://www.unchs.org.

14. Peter Hall and Ulrich Pfeiffer (eds), *Urban Future 21: A Global Agenda for Twenty-First Century Cities*, E. & F. N. Spon, London, 2000.

chapter 14: the role of British mission agencies and dioceses in international development

1. The current PWM mission agencies are: Church Army; Church's Ministry among Jewish People (CMJ); Church Mission Society (CMS); Crosslinks; Intercontinental Church Society; Mid-Africa Ministry (CMS); Missions to Seafarers; Mothers' Union; South American Mission Society (SAMS); Society for Promoting Christian Knowledge (SPCK); and United Society for the Propagation of the Gospel (USPG).

2. The Churches Commission on Mission (CCOM) is one of the permanent commissions established by Churches Together in Britain and Ireland (CTBI).

3. Formerly known as the Evangelical Missionary Alliance (EMA).

4. Following the celebration of its bicentenary in 1999 the CMS has written into its ten-year corporate plan the investigation of the implications of its adoption of one or all of the three concepts of decentralization, internationalization and regionalization.

5. See for example Samuel Escobar, *Missionary Dynamism in Search of Missiological Discernment*, Evangelical Review of Theology, 1999.

6. The reference here is to societies where the theological presuppositions of Hinduism or Buddhism are the controlling influence on individual and community world views.

7. Christians Aware is one example of a number of newer organizations that have focused on cross-cultural encounter and reflection as a powerful tool for moulding Christian understanding and response. Another such organization is Living Stones.

8. Most Church of England dioceses now have Companion Diocesan Links in one form or another. One area of concern, however, for the Church of England as a whole is that the majority of these links are with areas of western Europe and Africa. Few links are with the least evangelized areas of the world and even fewer with the non-Anglophone world. It is also disappointing that within dioceses there are sometimes poor links between the Companion Links and international development structures.

9. CMS, for example, launched its Praxis programme of overseas experience programmes for adults in 2000.

10. The distinction between these two words is much debated. Here I define evangelism as the process whereby a person or community is exposed to the gospel of Jesus Christ and invited to respond. Evangelization I define as the more comprehensive process that begins with cultural engagement, moves through evangelism, and continues with discipleship training and societal transformation.

11. The five marks of mission adopted by the Anglican Consultative Council following the Lambeth Conference of 1988 are: (1) To proclaim the good news of the kingdom; (2) To teach, baptize and nurture new believers; (3) To respond to human need by loving service; (4) To seek to transform unjust structures of society; and (5) To strive to safeguard the integrity of creation and sustain and renew the earth.

12. David Bosch, *Transforming Mission*, Orbis Books, New York, 1991.

13. Bryant Myers, *Walking with the Poor*, Orbis Books, New York, 1999, p. 88.

14. Walter Wink, *Engaging the Powers*, Fortress Press, Minneapolis, 1992, was the last of the trilogy and the most relevant for our current study.

15. Miroslav Volf, *Exclusion and Embrace*, Abingdon Press, Nashville, 1996.

16. Miroslav Volf, *Exclusion and Embrace*, p. 125.

17. David Meadows (ed.), *The Limits to Growth*, Pan Books, 1972; Jan Tinbergen, *Reshaping the International Order*, Dutton, NY, 1977; Willy Brandt, *North–South: A Programme for Survival*, MIT Press, Cambridge, Mass., 1980.

18. General Synod, *Development Education for the Church of England: A Report by the Board for Social Responsibility*, Church House Publishing, London, 1983.

19. John Taylor, *The Go-Between God*, OUP, Oxford, 1972.

20. General Synod, *Let Justice Flow: A Report by the Board for Social Responsibility*, Church House Publishing, London, 1986.

21. The Salisbury–Sudan link has a major funding element within it which puts it on a par with the smaller mission agencies, whereas the focus of the Winchester–Uganda link is much more clearly the building of understanding and personal support through visits and exchanges. The Derby–North India link is fully ecumenical, and Lichfield is part of a tripartite link that has had a significant youth exchange element built into it.

22. After finishing this chapter, I was pleased to learn that One World Week had secured significant funding from the Department for International Development. Its financial future appears secure, at least in the short term.

chapter 15: Christian Aid and the Church of England

1. For a copy of Christian Aid's 2000 vision statement, please contact Christian Aid, Inter-Church House, 35–41 Lower Marsh, London SE1 7RL.

2. Christian Aid, *Corporate Plan, 2000–2004*, Christian Aid, London, 2000, p. 2.

contacts

The Board for Social Responsibility	Church House, Great Smith Street, Westminster, London SW1 3NZ Tel: 020 7898 1000
CAFOD	Romero Close, Stockwell Road, London SW9 9TY Tel: 020 7733 7900
Catholic Institute for International Relations	Unit 3 Canonbury Yard, 190a New North Road, Islington, London N1 7BJ Tel: 020 7354 0883
Christian Aid	PO Box 100, London SE1 7RT Tel: 020 7620 4444
Church Army	Independents Road, Blackheath, London SE3 9LG Tel: 020 8318 1226
Churches Together in Britain and Ireland	Inter-Church House, 35–41 Lower Marsh, London SE1 7SA Tel: 020 7523 2121
Church's Ministry among Jewish People (CMJ)	30c Clarence Road, St Albans, Herts AL 4JJ Tel: 01727 833114
Church Mission Society (CMS)	Partnership House, 157 Waterloo Road, London SE1 8UU Tel: 020 7928 8681
Crosslinks	251 Lewisham Way, London SE4 1XF Tel: 020 8691 6111
Department for International Development	94 Victoria Street, London SW1E 5JL Tel: 020 7917 7000

Fair Trade Foundation   115 Southwark Bridge Road, London SE1 0AH
Tel: 020 7450 9050

Friends of the Earth   26–28 Underwood Street, London N1 7JQ
Tel: 020 7490 1555

Intercontinental   1 Athena Drive, Tachbrook Park, Warwick CV34 6NL
Church Society (ICS)   Tel: 01926 430347

Methodist Relief and   25 Marylebone Road, London NW1 5JR
Development Fund   Tel: 020 7486 5502

Mid-Africa Ministry   Partnership House, 157 Waterloo Road, London SE1 8UU
(CMS) – (MAM)   Tel: 020 7261 1370

Mission to Seafarers   St Michael Paternoster Royal, College Hill, London
EC4R 2RL
Tel: 020 7248 5202

Mothers' Union   Mary Sumner House, 24 Tufton Street, London
SW1P 3RB
Tel: 020 7222 5333

One World Week   PO Box 2555, Reading RG1 4XW
Tel: 0118 939 4933

Oxfam   Oxfam House, 274 Banbury Road, Oxford OX2 7DZ
Tel: 01865 311311

Religious Education   Rodwell House, Middlesex Street, London E1 7HJ
and Environment   Tel: 020 7377 0604
Programme

Society for Promoting   Holy Trinity Church, Marylebone Road, London NW1 4DU
Christian Knowledge   Tel: 020 7387 5282
(SPCK)

South American   Allen Gardiner House, 12 Fox Hill, Selly Oak, Birmingham
Mission Society   B29 4AG
(SAMS)   Tel: 0121 472 2616

Tearfund	100 Church Road, Teddington, Middlesex TW11 8QE Tel: 020 8977 9144
Tradecraft and Exchange	Kingsway, Gateshead, Tyne and Wear NE11 0NE Tel: 0191 491 0591
United Society for the Propagation of the Gospel (USPG)	Partnership House, 157 Waterloo Road, London SE1 8XA Tel: 020 7928 8681
World Development Movement	25 Beehive Place, London SW9 7QR Tel: 020 7737 6215
World Faiths Development Dialogue	33–37 Stockmore Street, Oxford OX4 1JJ Tel: 01865 790011

index